My Covenant

Realizing the urgency of the times,
the rapid fulfillment of Bible prophecy,
and my personal and our church's need for revival and reformation . . .

BY GOD'S GRACE AND HIS ENABLING POWER . . .

- **I will** prayerfully **STUDY** THE BIBLE and the Spirit of Prophecy writings each day.
- **I will** earnestly **PRAY** daily for the promised POWER of the HOLY SPIRIT for revival, reformation, and the final harvest.
- **I will** joyfully **SHARE** with others at every opportunity MY EXPERIENCE WITH CHRIST, the changes His love has brought to my life, and the hope He gives for the future.
- **I will** lovingly **SERVE** JESUS CHRIST as my Lord and Saviour and by His power prepare my life for His soon return!

Name ______________________ Date ____________

GETTING READY TO MEET JESUS

REVIEW AND HERALD® PUBLISHING ASSOCIATION
HAGERSTOWN, MD 21740

The author assumes full responsibility for the accuracy of all facts and quotations as cited in this book.

This book was
Edited by Gerald Wheeler and Bill Cleveland
Copyedited by Bill Cleveland and James Cavil
Designed by Bill Kirstein
Electronic Make-up by Shirley M. Bolivar
Cover illustrations by Clyde Provonsha
Interior illustrations by Art Landerman
Typeset: 11/12 Garamond

PRINTED IN U.S.A.

02 01 00 99 5 4 3 2

R&H Cataloging Service
Getting ready to meet Jesus.

1. Second Advent.
236

ISBN 0-8280-1410-8

Contents

Foreword

The prayer of Jesus on behalf of His people is particularly poignant today: "My prayer is not that you take them out of the world but that you protect them from the evil one. They are not of the world, even as I am not of it. Sanctify them by the truth; your word is truth" (John 17:15-17, NIV).

The head-spinning fulfillment of end-time prophecies as the world about us spirals toward moral, economic, environmental, and spiritual catastrophe can bring only sober reflection on that prayer to those who are "getting ready for Jesus."

Although as Seventh-day Adventists our little world may be somewhat insulated, we live in the very midst of a society saturated by materialism, secularism, and relativism, and are not immune to those ungodly and anti-God attitudes and mores.

Is it any wonder that our Lord sought the Father to "sanctify them by the truth"—the Word? That prayer, however, can be answered only as we make use of that which our great God has made available for that purpose—the Scriptures. And is it any wonder that He provided a special messenger for these times who would constantly call His church back to study His Word and provide illumination on that Word?

It is likely that there has never been a time in the history of the world when God's people had a greater need to be "sanctified" by the Word. Note this appeal made by our prophet, Ellen White, writing in the *Advent Review and Sabbath Herald,* published November 22, 1892: "Let everyone who claims to believe that the Lord is soon coming search the Scriptures as never before; for Satan is determined to try every device possible to keep souls in darkness, and blind the mind to the perils of the times in which we are living."

Won't you join us in resolving that the study of Scripture and the reading of God's special messages for these last days through the Spirit of Prophecy will occupy a central place in our lives as we get ready for Jesus?

AL and FRANCES McCLURE

Acknowledgments

This book has been developed by a special North American Division spiritual emphasis committee set up to explore ways to renew the church's study of the Bible and the Spirit of Prophecy. A number of its members contributed to the book's contents. Members of the committee as well as contributors include: Ed Reid, Calvin Smith, Bill Crofton, Cyril Miller, Jim Nix, Ruthie Jacobsen, Harold Lee, George Rice, Doug Sayles, Robert Smith, and Ted N. C. Wilson.

A special thanks goes to all who were involved in its preparation.

Realizing the urgency of the times,
the rapid fulfillment of Bible prophecy,
and my personal and our church's need for revival and reformation . . .

BY GOD'S GRACE AND HIS ENABLING POWER . . .

- **I will** prayerfully **STUDY** THE BIBLE and the Spirit of Prophecy writings each day.

- **I will** earnestly **PRAY** daily for the promised POWER of the HOLY SPIRIT for revival, reformation, and the final harvest.

- **I will** joyfully **SHARE** with others at every opportunity MY EXPERIENCE WITH CHRIST, the changes His love has brought to my life, and the hope He gives for the future.

- **I will** lovingly **SERVE** JESUS CHRIST as my Lord and Saviour and by His power prepare my life for His soon return!

Name ______________________________ Date ____________

INTRODUCTION

Our Need of God

As Seventh-day Adventist believers, we recognize the graciousness and love of God in sending His Son, Jesus, to die for us while we were yet sinners. Both as a church and as individuals we sense our spiritual inadequacy and the urgency of these last days of earth's history. We acknowledge the fact that we have not submitted ourselves fully to God's will and His plans for this church and our personal lives.

Recognizing that whenever the Word of God becomes the focal point in life it leads to spiritual revival, we seek a renewed emphasis on, and prayerful study of, the Bible. As we approach the second coming of Christ we need a new-birth experience of total submission to our Father's will. We want to become part of His proclamation of the Great Commission through the Advent movement.

Freely and gratefully we enter into a covenant relationship with Christ for the purpose of preparing ourselves, through the power of the Holy Spirit, to receive the latter-rain experience. Meeting with Christ every day through prayer, we ask for the infilling of the Holy Spirit through careful Bible study and through an earnest review of the Spirit of Prophecy. It is our desire, through an understanding and relationship gained by study and prayer, and empowered by the Holy Spirit, to lean completely on God. Through His power we will joyfully keep His law, live in harmony with His high standards, and support the fundamental beliefs of the remnant church.

It is important to make such a covenant with God concerning our loving service to Him and our complete dependence on Him. Israel offers us a powerful example to follow: "And because of all this we make a sure covenant, and write it; and our leaders and our Levites and our priests seal it" (Neh. 9:38). God's messenger to His remnant church also comments on this experience: "Then the whole congregation entered into a covenant to keep all the commandments of God; and that the transaction might be as effectual as possible, this covenant was written out, and those who were thoroughly in earnest in the work of reformation affixed their names and seals. . . .

"It would be a scene well-pleasing to God and angels, would His professed followers in this generation unite, as did Israel of old, in a solemn covenant to 'observe and do all the commandments of the Lord our Lord, and His judgments and His statutes'" *(Southern Watchman,* June 7, 1904).

Our Spirit-led return to primitive godliness will produce a revival that will enable us to lead those entrusted to our care into the latter-rain experience. As God presents opportunities, it will be our privilege to witness personally to others of our faith in Christ. Joyfully we commit ourselves to Christ.

By God's Grace and His Enabling Power

GOD'S WONDERFUL LOVE AND PLAN OF SALVATION—CENTERED IN CHRIST

Earth's history is reaching its culmination. Both Bible prophecy and the events taking place assure us that Jesus is coming soon! Although, as the Bible indicates, we may not know exactly when, we do know that the signs point to His imminent return. What a privilege it will be to see Jesus and be with Him forever! As Seventh-day Adventists, part of God's great Advent movement, we should be foremost in lifting up Christ to those around us as the only answer to the problems we all face. Christ, His wonderful love, and His plan of salvation should be the focus of all that we do. He and His righteousness should be the center of our witness as we share the good news of His soon return. Through His love, grace, and enabling power we have the opportunity to live for Him.

Sons and Daughters

John proclaimed, "Behold, what manner of love the Father has bestowed on us, that we should be called children of God!" (1 John 3:1). Through Jesus Christ we have the privilege of being God's sons and daughters. The grace of God, freely provided for His creatures, will bring us into a close relationship with Him. What a joyous privilege to know Jesus and His grace, to accept by faith His wonderful plan of salvation, and to allow Him to work in our lives through the Holy Spirit! Scripture assures us that "he who has the Son has life; he who does not have the Son of God does not have life. These things I have written to you who believe in the name of the Son of God, that you may know that you have eternal life" (1 John 5:12, 13). This is truly a demonstration of God's great love for His created beings.

Wonderful Plan

The Godhead, out of Their infinite love, established the plan of salvation even before humanity's creation and fall. God made this wondrous provision for our salvation at the cost of the life of His Son, the Creator Himself. "The Son of God, heaven's glorious Commander, was touched with pity for the fallen race. His heart was moved with infinite compassion as the woes of the lost world rose up before Him. But divine love had conceived a plan whereby man might be redeemed. The broken law of God demanded the life of the sinner. In all the universe there was but one who could, in behalf of man, satisfy its claims. Since the divine law is as sacred as God Himself, only one equal with God could make atonement for its transgression. None but Christ could redeem fallen man from the curse of the law and bring him again into harmony with Heaven. Christ would take upon Himself the guilt and shame of sin—sin so offensive to a holy God that it must separate the Father and His Son. Christ would reach to the depths of misery to rescue the ruined race" *(Patriarchs and Prophets,* p. 63). No wonder John exclaimed, "What manner of love."

Eternal Life Through Christ

It is a tremendous privilege to know that God loves us (John 3:16; Rom. 5:8); that though we are all sinners (Rom. 3:23), He provided us a remedy for sin (John

1:12; 1 Cor. 15:3, 4). Romans 6:23 indicates: "For the wages of sin is death, but the gift of God is eternal life in Christ Jesus our Lord." Only through Jesus Christ may we obtain a lease on eternal life. "Nothing but repentance toward God and faith in Christ can save the sinner. The grace of Christ cannot be purchased; it is a free gift" *(The Great Controversy,* p. 129).

Free Love, Free Choice

Our Creator and Redeemer enables each one of us of our own free choice to either accept or reject His gift of salvation. *Patriarchs and Prophets* declares that "the law of love being the foundation of the government of God, the happiness of all intelligent beings depends upon their perfect accord with its great principles of righteousness. God desires from all His creatures the service of love—service that springs from an appreciation of His character. He takes no pleasure in forced obedience; and to all He grants freedom of will, that they may render Him voluntary service" (p. 34).

Through faith in Christ and His sacrifice we may have a restored connection with God. Revelation 3:20 describes Christ as knocking at the door of our heart, inviting us to have fellowship with Him. He wants us to trust in Him. "For 'whoever calls upon the name of the Lord shall be saved' " (Rom. 10:13). As we depend totally upon Christ and His grace, we can have the assurance of being made right with God (Rom. 10:9; John 5:24; 1 John 5:13; John 20:31). We may have heaven's peace as we rely upon Christ's righteousness and power. Romans 5:1, 2 indicates that "having been justified by faith, we have peace with God through our Lord Jesus Christ, through whom also we have access by faith into this grace in which we stand, and rejoice in hope of the glory of God."

Jesus Christ Our All in All

When we accept Jesus through the power of the Holy Spirit, He not only justifies us, but gives us the power to become more and more like Him through sanctification. "But as many as received Him, to them He gave the right to become children of God, even to those who believe in His name: who were born, not of blood, nor of the will of the flesh, nor of the will of man, but of God" (John 1:12, 13). "Let the subject be made distinct and plain that it is not possible to effect anything in our standing before God or in the gift of God to us through creature merit" *(Faith and Works,* pp. 19, 20). We are to look to Christ and live—to grow in Him by His grace and enabling power. Once we realize that we have salvation only in Christ and His righteousness, we will praise Him and give Him the glory for His incredible gift!

Salvation in Christ

When we daily accept Christ, we open ourselves to the entire salvation process. Christ both justifies (Rom. 5:1, 2) us through His sacrificial death and sanctifies (1 Thess. 5:23) us through His righteous life. At all times we must depend completely upon Christ. He is the source of our salvation and life, both now and in the future. Christ has made possible the only way of escape from sin and this earth.

In His Service

Focusing on Jesus, the author and finisher of our faith, will create in us a tremendous urge to serve Him. "Looking at the cross of Calvary, you will have a desire to bear the cross" *(Faith and Works,* p. 16). It will be our privilege to serve the Lord and become increasingly like Him in our love and service to others. At the same time, the more we look to Christ, the more we will see our need of Him. "Those who are really seeking to perfect Christian character will never indulge the thought that they are sinless. Their lives may be irreproachable, they may be living representatives of the truth which they have accepted; but the more they discipline their minds to dwell upon the character of Christ, and the nearer they approach to His divine image, the more clearly will they discern its spotless perfection, and the more deeply will they feel their own defects. . . . While with penitence and humble trust we meditate upon Jesus, whom our sins have pierced and our sorrows have burdened, we may learn to walk in His footsteps. By beholding Him we become changed into His divine likeness. And when this work is wrought in us, we shall claim no righteousness of our own, but shall exalt Jesus Christ, while we hang our helpless souls upon His merits. . . . True sanctification is an entire conformity to the will of God. Rebellious thoughts and feelings are overcome, and the voice of Jesus awakens a new life, which pervades the entire being. . . . True sanctification is a daily work, continuing as long as life shall last. Those who are battling with daily temptations, overcoming their own sinful tendencies, and seeking for holiness of heart and life, make no boastful claims of holiness. They are hungering and thirsting for righteousness" *(The Sanctified Life,* pp. 7-10).

**The Beautiful Balance of the Salvation Process—
Christ's Grace and Enabling Power**

Steps to Christ offers an in-depth understanding of Christ's salvation and His power to save. The chapter entitled "The Test of Discipleship" details the scope and extent of Christ's grace and enabling power. It presents in a powerful way the beautiful balance of His justification and sanctification. "The condition of eternal life is now just what it always has been—just what it was in Paradise before the fall of our first parents—perfect obedience to the law of God, perfect righteousness. If eternal life were granted on any condition short of this, then the happiness of the whole universe would be imperiled. The way would be open for sin, with all its train of woe and misery, to be immortalized.

"It was possible for Adam, before the fall, to form a righteous character by obedience to God's law. But he failed to do this, and because of his sin our natures are fallen and we cannot make ourselves righteous. Since we are sinful, unholy, we cannot perfectly obey the holy law. We have no righteousness of our own with which to meet the claims of the law of God. But Christ has made a way of escape for us. He lived on earth amid trials and temptations such as we have to meet. He lived a sinless life. He died for us, and now He offers to take our sins and give us His righteousness. If you give yourself to Him, and accept Him as your Saviour, then, sinful as your life may have been, for His sake you are accounted righteous. Christ's character stands in place of your character, and you are accepted before God just as if you had not sinned.

"More than this, Christ changes the heart. He abides in your heart by faith. You are to maintain this connection with Christ by faith and the continual surrender of your will to Him; and so long as you do this, He will work in you to will and to do according to His good pleasure. So you may say, 'The life which I now live in the flesh I live by the faith of the Son of God, who loved me, and gave himself for me' (Gal. 2:20, KJV). So Jesus said to His disciples, 'It is not ye that speak, but the Spirit of your Father which speaketh in you' (Matt. 10:20, KJV). Then with Christ working in you, you will manifest the same spirit and do the same good work—works of righteousness, obedience.

"So we have nothing in ourselves of which to boast. We have no ground for self-exaltation. Our only ground of hope is in the righteousness of Christ imputed to us, and in that wrought by His Spirit working in and through us" (pp. 62, 63).

Preparation for Christ's Soon Second Coming Through His Grace and Enabling Power

We have a marvelous plan of salvation from a marvelous Saviour! What a privilege to accept His grace and enabling power to prepare us to meet Him at His imminent second coming! As we give Him our hearts, our praise, and our service, Jesus Christ should mean everything to us. Let us speak of Him, share Him with others. We can sum up the Holy Spirit's power to enable us to live for Him in these beautiful thoughts: "The greatest praise that men can bring to God is to become consecrated channels through whom He can work. Time is rapidly passing into eternity. Let us not keep back from God that which is His own. Let us not refuse Him that which, though it cannot be given without merit, cannot be denied without ruin. He asks for a whole heart; give it to Him; it is His, both by creation and by redemption. He asks for your intellect; give it to Him; it is His. He asks for your money; give it to Him; it is His. 'Ye are not your own, for ye are bought with a price' (1 Cor. 6:19, 20). God requires the homage of a sanctified soul, which has prepared itself, by the exercise of the faith that works by love, to serve Him. He holds up before us the highest ideal, even perfection. He asks us to be absolutely and completely for Him in this world as He is for us in the presence of God. . . . Desire the fullness of the grace of Christ. Let your heart be filled with an intense longing for His righteousness, the work of which God's Word declares is peace, and its effect quietness and assurance forever. As your soul yearns after God, you will find more and still more of the unsearchable riches of His grace. As you contemplate these riches you will come into possession of them and will reveal the merits of the Saviour's sacrifice, the protection of His righteousness, the fullness of His wisdom, and His power to present you before the Father 'without spot, and blameless' (2 Peter 3:14, KJV)" *(The Acts of the Apostles,* pp. 566, 567).

COVENANT ONE

"I Will Prayerfully Study the Bible and the Spirit of Prophecy Writings Each Day"

HOW TO STUDY THE BIBLE

The Bible is the Word of God. It is alive (Heb. 4:12), it is the source of all truth (John 17:17), and it contains power to change lives (John 6:63). When we open the Bible, we hear the voice of God. Following are some suggestions to help make your Bible study more meaningful.

Proper Frame of Mind

With the Bible in hand, we stand in the presence of God. Its words came from the pens of chosen individuals inspired by the Holy Spirit (2 Tim. 3:16). From its pages God speaks, and we are to listen.

Therefore, we should read and study the Bible with the humble spirit of one who desires to learn. The self-reliance that scientists bring to their fields of study is not to be the attitude with which a human being approaches the fountain of spiritual truth. "We must come with a humble and teachable spirit to obtain knowledge from the great I AM" *(The Great Controversy,* p. 599).

Because spiritual truths are spiritually discerned,

we must keep the channels of communication open so the Holy Spirit can bring conviction concerning biblical truth. We should try to avoid thinking of secular matters while reading the Bible. If our attention begins to wander into life's affairs, we must refocus and reread to pick up any thoughts that we may have missed. Feeding our minds with the excitement of TV drama and violence, or putting our nerves on edge as a result of chemical stimulants taken into the body, will prevent us from grasping the spiritual truths of Scripture.

Choose a proper time and place to study the Word of God. When our minds are rested and alert, the Word will make its deepest impressions. Read the Bible in a place free of distractions. In the quietness of our own thoughts, we will be able to hear the voice that speaks from the sacred pages: "Be still, and know that I am God" (Ps. 46:10).

One of the most effective ways to encourage regular study of both Scripture and the Spirit of Prophecy is through family worship. Ellen White tells us that "in arousing and strengthening a love for Bible study, much depends on the use of the hour of worship. The hours of morning and evening worship should be the sweetest and most helpful in the day" *(My Life Today,* p. 30). The family comes together as a whole to study God's Word.

Families with young children could use some of the recent translations especially geared to children, such as the *International Children's Bible.* As the children become older, the family can read from adult translations so they can become used to the cadence and beauty of the language.

Always parents should encourage the whole family to discuss what they have just read from the Bible. Ellen

White tells us that we should ask questions about the passage *(Testimonies,* vol. 7, p. 43). We should try to make Scripture as practical as possible, sharing with each other what the biblical stories, promises, and admonitions mean in our daily life. If children do not understand something they find in the Bible, we must encourage them to ask about it, then help them to look up background material and suggestions from good commentaries and other resources.

Family worship is also a good time to read from the Spirit of Prophecy. For younger children we can select passages from the Conflict of the Ages Series, especially focusing on the narrative parts. They will especially enjoy *The Story of Jesus,* a book that was adapted from Ellen White's *Desire of Ages.* Other times we might use a topical approach to Ellen White's writings to look at subjects that we as a family might be interested in at the moment. But whatever we do, we must avoid using our readings from her writings as a form of discipline or punishment for something our children might have done. This will only create a negative impression in their minds toward the Spirit of Prophecy.

With the proper attitude, reading the Bible can make a profound change in our lives. "There is nothing more calculated to strengthen the intellect than the study of the Scriptures. No other book is so potent to elevate the thoughts, to give vigor to the faculties, as the broad, ennobling truths of the Bible" *(Steps to Christ,* p. 90).

Pray

The study of God's Word should always begin with prayer. We may invite the same Holy Spirit who inspired the Bible writers to fill our minds with His presence and open our understanding to what we are about to read. Always we must ask Him to give us the attitude of a learner, the humility of one willing to be taught. As we study, it is beneficial to pause often and talk to God about what we have just read. If it is a promise, we may personalize the promise by thanking Him for it. Or if it is instruction, we may ask Him to apply it to our lives. And if it is a warning, let us request strength to profit from the admonition. Our reading and study should take the form of a two-way conversation.

Beginning Where We Are Comfortable

For beginners, the easiest place to start reading the Bible is with the life of Jesus, especially as presented in the Gospel of John. Then branch out into the other Gospels to obtain a fuller picture of His life and ministry. Eventually, we will feel comfortable no matter where we read. History buffs will enjoy the five books written by Moses, the history of Israel and the lives of its kings, and in the New Testament, the lives and deeds of the apostles. Lovers of poetry will thrill to the Psalms and the book of Job. Those with a philosophical bent will gladly immerse themselves in Proverbs and Ecclesiastes. Romantics will turn to the Song of Solomon. Those interested in prophecy will find that Daniel, Revelation, and the classical prophets of the Old Testament speak equally to them. The New Testament Epistles have much to say about the practical matters of life. From wherever we begin, we must next branch out into the other books of the Bible. We may be pleasantly surprised to find that we are less uncomfortable delving into Scripture than we first expected.

Use a Concordance

As the Holy Spirit impresses us with the importance of a particular subject, a concordance will allow us to find other passages of Scripture that will bring added information to our study. When we encounter apparent contradictions, we must not jump to conclusions. Rather we should reserve judgment until we can gather more information. Because the Holy Spirit inspired all that the Bible contains, all of its teachings are consistent. We need only be patient and let the Spirit guide our minds in resolving what appear to be inconsistencies. Using a concordance to find other passages relating to a given topic can help in solving problems.

Most concordances simply help us locate other verses of Scripture that complement the particular word or thought that is of interest. Specialized concordances, such as *Strong's Concordance,* are more detailed and are designed to aid in deeper study. They will supply the Hebrew or Greek word that lies behind the English word you are interested in. For example, should the English word "crown" in the New Testament catch our eye, we will discover that the *diadēma* (Greek, translated crowns) on the seven heads of the great red dragon in Revelation 12:3 and the many crowns Jesus wears in Revelation 19:12 are distinguished from the *stephanos* (Greek, translated crown) worn by the woman clothed in the sun in Revelation 12:1, 2.

Once we have information from a more detailed concordance and wish further information, we may refer to such works as A. T. Robertson's *Word Pictures in the New Testament*. We will discover that the crown worn by the woman of Revelation 12 is a chaplet usually made of some type of vegetation and is a symbol of victory. Ironically, the crown of thorns placed upon Jesus' head in a gesture of mockery was a *stephanos*—in reality, a symbol of victory. The crowns worn by Jesus in

Revelation 19 are blue ribbons embroidered in white and introduced by the Persian kings to hold the royal turban securely in place. Such blue ribbons themselves became a symbol of royalty, and it is from *diadēma* that we get the English word diadem. Because a *diadēma* is a ribbon, the reader can now understand how Jesus can wear "many" of them at the same time.

Memorize

We can enhance our memory and strengthen our spiritual life by memorizing favorite verses and passages of Scripture. Then portions of God's Word will always be with us to be called upon when needed for comfort and strength. Such passages committed to memory form a line of defense against Satan's deceptions. God's people have been assured that "none but those who have fortified the mind with the truths of the Bible will stand through the last great conflict" *(The Great Controversy,* pp. 593, 594).

For starters, memorize the Psalms. They were composed to be sung, and therefore lend themselves to easy memorization. The Gospel of Mark can be easily memorized. Some feel that Mark may have been among a select group that had committed the deeds and teachings of Jesus to memory so they could teach others and prepare them for entrance into the early church.

Let the Bible Speak for Itself

We must not force Scripture to say what we want. To get the true meaning from a Bible passage, we should take the obvious meaning of the words unless they clearly employ a symbol or figure of speech.

When the Bible employs such a figure, it will explain what that imagery represents. Sometimes we can find its meaning in the immediate context. For example, in Revelation 17:1 we read about the "great harlot who sits on many waters." In verse 15 of the same chapter, John explains that the waters represent "peoples" (i.e., nations). If we go back to the great red dragon of Revelation 12:3, 4, we will discover in verse 9 that the imagery represents Satan. In the cases of the water and the dragon, John tells us right up front what they stand for.

The immediate context may not identify some symbols, nor are we told plainly what they mean. In such cases other Bible books help us to understand what the symbol means by the way they use the symbol. For example, Revelation introduces the reader to two women—one "clothed with the sun" (Rev. 12:1, 2) and the other dressed in scarlet and "drunk with the blood of the saints" (Rev. 17:4-6). The reader learns from Old Testament imagery that a woman represents a religious group or a church (Ps. 9:14). Therefore, the woman clothed in the sun in Revelation 12 represents God's faithful people, while the woman clothed in scarlet in Revelation 17 represents an apostate church.

We should beware of trying to wring future dates out of time periods mentioned in the Bible. Rather make sure you keep time prophecies within their context. For example, the time periods found in Daniel 9:24-27 give meaning to the 2300-year prophecy of Daniel 8:14. In Daniel 9 each reference to time made by the angel occurs within the context of the 2300-year period. We must not try to force the 69 weeks and the 70 weeks to indicate something that does not relate to the 2300 years.

So remember, do not try to force a prophetic date out of a historical/chronological period of time. Chronological time is chronological time, and prophetic time is prophetic time. The Bible will make clear which is which. If we are honest in the way we read Scripture, the Holy Spirit will surely richly reward our efforts to understand.

Guides to Bible Study

The most popular guide for the study of the Bible in the Seventh-day Adventist Church is the Sabbath school quarterly. These guides are generally topical, leading the reader through one subject at a time. But guides offer the opportunity for more extensive reading if you want to understand the context in which a passage appears. Extending the reading beyond a single verse or two gives a deeper insight into the topic under consideration. With this preparation, the Sabbath school class discussion will center on what the Bible teaches on a given subject and not on people's opinions of the subject.

Such Bible handbooks as Mark Finley's *Studying Together* can be very useful for topical Bible study as well as providing a ready reference for answering questions on Bible subjects. But for the feeding and strengthening of the spiritual life, nothing replaces the unhurried reading of large passages of Scripture in one sitting—four or five chapters or the complete reading of a smaller book, interspersed with frequent prayer asking God for understanding and strength to live by His Word.

HOW TO STUDY THE SPIRIT OF PROPHECY

During Ellen White's lifetime (1827-1915) one writer compared her writings to a telescope and the truths of Scripture to stars in the sky. The telescope does not project new stars into the heavens, but focuses on and enhances the visibility of some stars that would otherwise be obscure. Ellen White always denied that her writings were on the same level as Scripture. From the beginning of her ministry until its close 70 years later, she exalted the Bible and urged people to study it. In her first book, published in 1851, she wrote: "I recommend to you, dear reader, the Word of God as the rule of your faith and practice. By that Word we are to be judged" *(Early Writings,* p. 78). "In His Word, God has committed to men the knowledge necessary for salvation. The Holy Scriptures are to be accepted as an authoritative, infallible revelation of His will. They are the standard of character, the revealer of doctrines, and the test of experience" *(The Great Controversy,* p. vii). In response to some who believed her writings to be an addition to the Bible, she declared: "You are not familiar with the Scriptures. If you had made God's Word your study, with a desire to reach the Bible standard and attain to Christian perfection, you would not have needed the *Testimonies" (Testimonies,* vol. 5, p. 664). "The Lord has given a lesser light," she wrote, "to lead men and women to the greater light" *(Colporteur Evangelist,* p. 37).

How to Begin

Studying the Spirit of Prophecy writings, like studying the Bible, is extremely personal. Different people will go about it in different ways. When we start, the single most important thing we can do is to ask ourselves, "What does God want to tell me as I read?" Only when we earnestly desire to know God's will for our life are we really ready to proceed to the next step, setting a specific time each day for doing our study. It may be early in the day or late, and it may be for only 15 minutes or an hour or more. But whatever we decide, we must get into the habit of spending a set amount of quality time each day in prayerful study.

So how do we begin? Ideally, we should start by reading one or more of the books Ellen White wrote during her lifetime. Depending upon our interests, we might begin with her very popular little devotional book *Steps to Christ*. From there we might go on to her classic biography of Christ, *The Desire of Ages*. Or we might choose to read Ellen White's earliest experiences, collected together in the book *Early Writings*.

Another possibility is to start with *Patriarchs and Prophets,* her volume that parallels the first part of the Old Testament. We then continue reading the four other books in her Conflict of the Ages series that trace the history of the great controversy between Christ and Satan from before Creation until the earth made new. If prophecy and last-day events interest us, Ellen White's *Great Controversy,* the last book in her five-volume series just mentioned, should be high on our reading list.

For readers who find Ellen White's nineteenth-century writing style difficult to understand, the books *Steps to Christ* and *The Story of Redemption* have been translated into easier English. Also, some of her other books have been condensed, though the words themselves have not been simplified. Use of such editions will be extremely helpful to those of us who want to know what Ellen White said, but have difficulty with the way she originally phrased her books.

After we have become familiar with Ellen White's spiritual emphasis and nineteenth-century writing style (or have read one of the more recent editions just described), we are now ready to move on in our study of her writings. Again, what we do next will depend pretty much upon the individual reader. Some will choose a book and just start reading. Others may want to purchase a study guide to aid in their reading. Such guides have been prepared for several of Ellen White's books. Still others may want to start a systematic reading plan that combines Scripture passages with parallel passages from the writings of Ellen White. *Correlated Bible Readings,* by Arl Voorheis, is an excellent help for this type of study plan.

Digging Deeper

As one studies deeper into the writings of Ellen White, several research tools will become increasingly helpful. The four-volume *Index to the Writings of Ellen G. White* opens up the possibility of doing topical studies into her writings. It is now also available on CD-ROM, as is the *Published Ellen G. White Writings on Compact Disc.* This latter CD-ROM contains all of Ellen White's known published writings.

Before proceeding too far into our reading plan we may want to avail ourselves of several excellent books that will help us better understand Ellen White and the times in which she lived. For starters, Herbert Douglass's *Messenger of the Lord* is a veritable gold mine of information regarding the life, ministry, and writings of Ellen White. Likewise, Arthur White's six-volume biography of Ellen G. White is an invaluable source both for biographical information as well as for the backgrounds of many of Ellen White's books and individual testimonies.

George Knight's two small, easy-to-read books, *Meeting Ellen White* and *Reading Ellen White*, are especially helpful introductory sources for new readers of the Spirit of Prophecy. They contain brief biographical information regarding Mrs. White and in-depth explanations on the great themes upon which she dwelled, as well as suggestions on how to study her writings. Since Ellen White lived mostly during the nineteenth century, you may also want to read George Knight's *Ellen White's World* or Gary Land's *World of Ellen White*. Both books will help you learn more about the times during which she lived.

Other informative books that contain background information about Ellen White's visions and testimonies include Roger Coon's *Great Visions of Ellen G. White* and Paul Gordon's *My Dear Brother M*. An especially helpful book on the subject of inspiration and its application to Ellen White's ministry is Juan Carlos Viera's *Voice of the Spirit*.

Adventists sometimes divide Ellen White's books into those she produced during her lifetime and those compiled from her various writings since her death in 1915. The latter group, often referred to simply as compilations, have been brought together from Mrs. White's letter and manuscript files in accordance with her will. However, dividing her books this way is too simplistic to be generally helpful when developing a meaningful study plan.

Your Study Approach

As you read Ellen White's books, it is often helpful to differentiate between those designed specifically for spiritual reading and those better suited for topical study. Which of the two categories a book fits in depends upon the type of material it contains. Many Spirit of Prophecy books were designed specifically to be read from cover to cover. In this category, besides the books already mentioned, are such volumes as *Education, The Ministry of Healing,* and *The Story of Redemption*. Others, including some compilations, are more encyclopedic in nature. Rather than having chapters that contain long sections from Mrs. White's writings, including the contexts from which the compilers took the selections, this category attempts to provide the reader with as much counsel from Ellen White as possible on a particular topic in a limited space. Consequently, quotations are often short and to the point, and are printed without their original context. Books of this type include *Counsels on Diet and Foods, Evangelism,* and *Temperance.*

In addition to the above two categories, a number of Ellen White devotional books contain short spiritual readings for every day of the year. Other devotional-type books, such as *Steps to Christ* and *The Sanctified Life,* also have short chapters for easy reading. Still another general category of books that contain practical counsel for the church are the nine volumes of *Testimonies for the Church,* as well as the three books of *Selected Messages.*

Topical Approach

Another approach to the Spirit of Prophecy is to divide the books according to the topics they cover. Following is a suggested topical list. While it does not contain every possible Ellen White book that might fit under each specific category, it does give most of the common titles.

AUTOBIOGRAPHY

Life Sketches of Ellen G. White, 1915
Spiritual Gifts, vol. 2 (bound with vol. 1), 1860

BIBLE STUDY

Acts of the Apostles, The, 1911
Christ's Object Lessons, 1900
Desire of Ages, The, 1898

Patriarchs and Prophets, 1890
Prophets and Kings, 1917
Sketches From the Life of Paul, 1883
Story of Redemption, The, 1947
Thoughts From the Mount of Blessing, 1896
Truth About Angels, The, 1996

CHURCH AND PASTORAL MINISTRY
Christian Service, 1925
Counsels on Sabbath School Work, 1938
Evangelism, 1946
Gospel Workers, 1915
Selected Messages (3 books), 1958-1980
Testimonies for the Church (9 vols.), 1885-1909
Welfare Ministry, 1952

DEVOTIONAL
Daughters of God, 1998
Faith I Live By, The, 1958
God Has Promised, 1982
In Heavenly Places, 1967
Maranatha, 1976
My Life Today, 1952
Our High Calling, 1961
Sanctified Life, The, 1937
Sons and Daughters of God, 1955
Steps to Christ, 1892
That I May Know Him, 1964
Ye Shall Receive Power, 1996

EDUCATION
Counsels to Parents, Teachers, and Students, 1913
Education, 1903
Fundamentals of Christian Education, 1923

HEALTH

Counsels on Diet and Foods, 1938
Counsels on Health, 1923
Medical Ministry, 1932
Ministry of Healing, The, 1905
Temperance, 1949

HOME AND FAMILY

Adventist Home, The, 1952
Child Guidance, 1954
Counsels on Stewardship, 1940
Letters to Young Lovers, 1983
Messages to Young People, 1930

LAST-DAY EVENTS

Great Controversy, The, 1888, revised 1911
Last-Day Events, 1992

MISCELLANEOUS

Early Writings, 1882
Ellen G. White Review and Herald Articles (6 vols.), 1962
Ellen G. White Signs of the Times Articles (4 vols.), 1974
Ellen G. White Youth's Instructor Articles, 1986

Guiding Principles for Studying the Spirit of Prophecy Writings

As any reader of the Spirit of Prophecy writings quickly discovers, Ellen White wrote on a variety of topics. That being so, the following guiding principles have been suggested for serious readers of her writings:

1. The Spirit of Prophecy writings are not given to take the place of faith, hard work, initiative, or Bible study.

2. Study the Spirit of Prophecy to find the counsels God has given, not just to prove our own conclusions.
3. The Spirit of Prophecy writings are intended as messages to me personally, not as a club to use on someone else.
4. Study all the counsels available on a given subject in order to gain the full picture of what God is trying to teach us through Ellen White's writings.
5. Conclusions based upon the study of the Spirit of Prophecy must be in harmony with all of the writings taken as a whole.
6. Study specific counsels in their setting. Take time and place into consideration. What may have been appropriate for one person may not fit another's situation at all. In using testimonies originally written to institutions or individuals, keep in mind that conditions may have changed. Also, the meaning of some words has changed through the years.
7. Although situations may change, since the underlying principles found in the Spirit of Prophecy are universal in application, seek to correctly understand those principles so that we can apply them to our own situation today.
8. God gives us in the Spirit of Prophecy writings an ideal for which we should strive. If we fall short in some respects, we should not become discouraged. It may take time for God to transform us. Thankfully, God does not reject or cast off His people if they come short of His ideal.
9. Be absolutely honest in relationship to the counsels found in the Spirit of Prophecy. Also, we

must be willing to acknowledge the influence of our own attitudes upon ourselves and others.

10. Apply the counsels contained in the Spirit of Prophecy consistently. We are not at liberty to accept part and reject the rest.
11. Be tolerant of others. Different people have come through different experiences and from different backgrounds. There are some things each of us must settle with our own conscience and with God. Also, recognize that God gives us opportunity for doubt if we wish to do so.
12. Read the Spirit of Prophecy counsels from Ellen White's books and not in someone's unauthorized photocopied collection or privately printed compilation.

In summary, adopt an attitude open toward God's leading when studying the Spirit of Prophecy; set a specific time each day to study; select a reading plan that meets your spiritual needs; and then prayerfully begin, knowing that God will bless you for having spent this meaningful time with Him.

THOUGHT QUESTIONS FOR

COVENANT ONE

How to Study the Bible

Ask Yourself . . .

• Which comes first, meaningful Bible study or a contrite heart?

• We tend to enjoy doing things we want to do. What might make us want to study the Bible? Consider the following: (1) our strong wish to be in harmony with God and at peace with ourselves; (2) our longing for good news in today's troubled world; (3) our curiosity at the future of humanity; (4) our trust that God speaks to us through His Word and provides the best answers to our questions.

• In John 6 Jesus calls Himself "the bread of life." If you were to compare the frequency and amount of your Bible study to your regular food intake, what would be the state of your spiritual health? Spiritually are you (1) healthy and full, (2) often hungry, (3) malnourished and listless, or (4) starving to the point of death?

• Especially for youth: Some people today consider the Bible to have lost its relevance because much of it describes the history of an ancient nation. Can you identify characteristics of human nature in Bible stories that suggest the error of this view? For examples, check out Genesis 18:15; Numbers 12; Joshua 7:20, 21; 1 Samuel 1:12-14; 2 Samuel 11; 12; Nehemiah 2:1-5; Esther 5:9, 10; Job 2:9, 10; Psalm 10; Proverbs 25:24; Daniel 6:18; Jonah 4:1-3.

How to Study the Spirit of Prophecy

Ask Yourself . . .

• One reviewer of Ellen White's writings wrote that she sounds like a country lawyer, suggesting that she communicated wisdom in a straightforward, even everyday, way. Considering that Ellen White had little formal schooling but wrote many influential books, where do you think the wisdom came from?

• Many individuals have taken small sections of Ellen White's writings and pasted them together to make theological assertions that she did not intend. How can we quote Ellen White responsibly and avoid this kind of imbalance?

• Ellen White's writings have been characterized by some as relevant to the author's century but not to ours. As we look toward the new millennium, how would we defend her canon as a relevant influence on contemporary society? Consider the following subjects as they are treated by Ellen White: the unchanging sin problem; God's unchanging salvation plan; signs of end-time prophecy fulfillment; our eternal future.

• Especially for youth: Ellen White struggled with feelings of inadequacy, spiritually and in other ways, as a teenager (see her descriptions in the first chapter of *Early Writings).* She saw herself as an ordinary person to whom God gave a special gift to share. Have you read an Ellen White book with the idea that it's a gift of reassurance to you?

"I Will Earnestly Pray Daily for the Promised Power of the Holy Spirit for Revival, Reformation, and the Final Harvest"

HOW TO PRAY
Enlarging Your Territory

Intercessory prayer gives us incredible possibilities for enlarging our territory of service. We may pray for someone in our own homes, next door, or halfway around the world, and God hears those prayers in heaven. The lives of those for whom we pray are influenced from above.

First Chronicles 4:10 mentions an honorable man of Judah named Jabez, and records a prayer he made: "And Jabez called on the God of Israel saying, 'Oh, that You would bless me indeed, and enlarge my territory, that Your hand would be with me, and that You would keep me from evil.'" So God granted what he requested.

Through prayer for others, our territory of service can be vast and limitless. Our prayers can reach anyone, anywhere, and because God hears and has promised to answer, wonderful things happen when we pray.

Prayer is one of the most unselfish and noble gifts we can give to another, because only God knows, and He alone receives the glory for the results.

Whether we are asking in prayer to know Him better, for Him to do something in the life of someone else, or for Him to provide for a tangible need, He longs to answer. "God delights to give. He is full of compassion, and He longs to grant the requests of those who come unto Him in faith. He gives to us that we may minister to others and thus become like Himself" *(Christ's Object Lessons,* p. 141).

He loves to have us approach Him as His children, expecting Him to hear and to answer, and He loves to have us call Him our Father. It makes the relationship more real in our minds. "He gives us the privilege of calling the infinite God our Father. This name, spoken to Him and of Him, is a sign of our love and trust toward Him, and a pledge of His regard and relationship to us. Spoken when asking His favor or blessing, it is as music in His ears" *(ibid.,* p. 142).

In the parable of the selfish neighbor Christ presented powerful prayer principles. He pointed out the importance of a true spirit in prayer, and the need for perseverance. And He taught that we are to ask from Him that we may give to others. Doing so changes our hearts and brings us into harmony with God. God is the greatest giver, and He wants us to learn from Him how we too can give in love to others.

In addition, "when we make requests of Him, He may see that it is necessary for us to search our hearts and repent of sin. Therefore He takes us through test and trial, He brings us through humiliation, that we may see what hinders the working of His Holy Spirit through us" *(ibid.,* p. 143).

In Old Testament times the Hebrew language had no word for impossible. Perhaps that was because God's people knew that if they were walking in obedience, there was nothing that He *couldn't* or *wouldn't* do for them. And today His answers are still promised on the basis of fulfilling His conditions of obedience. But He gives the conditions as guidelines, not to discourage, but to point the way. "All His gifts are promised on condition of obedience. God has a heaven full of blessings for those who will cooperate with Him. All who obey Him may with confidence claim the fulfillment of His promises" *(ibid.,* p. 145).

Our Father wants us to trust Him and to know that He is trustworthy. James tells us that we need to ask without hesitation. Abraham believed God, and as a result, Scripture calls him God's friend. "Prayer and faith are closely allied, and they need to be studied together" *(Messages to Young People,* p. 252). "Often He delays to answer us in order to try our faith or test the genuineness of our desire. Having asked according to His Word, we should believe His promise and press our petitions with a determination that will not be denied" *(Christ's Object Lessons,* p. 145).

The chapter "Asking to Give" in the book *Christ's Object Lessons* gives us wonderful gems of truth. There we're told that when we have difficulties, our very first thought should be to pray. "Trust all with God. The practice of telling our difficulties to others only makes us weak, and brings no strength to them" *(ibid.,* p. 146).

Who hasn't wished for more wisdom, direction, information, or help in critical situations? Here is a statement that brings great hope:

"It is not the capabilities you now possess or ever will have that will give you success. It is that which the

Lord can do for you. We need to have far less confidence in what man can do and far more confidence in what God can do for every believing soul. He longs to have you reach after Him by faith. He longs to have you expect great things from Him" *(ibid.,* p. 146).

But *how* do we carry out the resolution to pray *more?* Many today spend one to three hours every day in prayer. How do they do that? Some have said they couldn't possibly find that much time, nor would they know how to spend that much time if they did have it.

Well, we can't find the time—we must *make it.* But when we commit ourselves to prayer and give God our time, He rewards in abundance. It's like paying tithe. Those who have never paid tithe don't understand that they can actually have more by giving at least a tenth to God. The more we give to Him, the more we have to give, and the more He blesses us in other ways. The same is true with our time. When we give Him our time, He makes the rest of the day more effective and efficient.

Although there are many different ways to pray, the important thing is to spend time, as Mary did, sitting at the feet of Jesus, learning, growing, having Him lead, yielding to His Lordship (see Luke 10:41, 42).

Some write their prayers. It is a marvelous way to keep our minds from wandering, to remain focused and on target. To our amazement, we soon discover the Holy Spirit Himself instructing our hearts. We'll find a communication between our souls and heaven that we have never experienced before.

Many prefer to pray silently. Others pray aloud. Some carry on conversations with God as they go about their daily activities. They talk to Him as to a guest who is physically present.

When we are praying, just as when walking or jogging, it helps to have a route to follow. The Lord's Prayer is an ideal structure and provides the organization to guide us through our prayer time. "In the Lord's Prayer we have an example of a perfect petition. How simple, yet how comprehensive it is! . . . Let all study carefully the principles contained in it" *(Review and Herald,* Jan. 3, 1907). By following a plan in prayer, prayer time will be more meaningful, and we will be able to talk to God about those things that are most vital in our lives and for those whom He places on our hearts. (A suggested outline using the Lord's Prayer appears later.)

Begin and end every prayer with praise. In Psalm 22 David tells us that God inhabits the praises of His people. As we come into His presence with praise and gratitude and worship, anxiety vanishes.

Another way to provide structure for our prayers is to follow the acronym ACTS—adoration, confession, thanksgiving, and supplication (requests). Each part of the prayer, when used with Scripture or song, becomes a rich time of transformation in His presence. "When we come to Him confessing our unworthiness and sin, He has pledged Himself to give heed to our cry. The honor of His throne is staked for the fulfillment of His word unto us" *(Christ's Object Lessons,* p. 148).

God changes us as we spend time in His presence. His Holy Spirit transforms us.

Perspectives on Prayer

As we seek for God's will in our prayer, we will find that through His power we will achieve our purposes, as He responds to our desires in His infinitely better way. He knows how to provide a better answer than we could ever possibly imagine. The Lord never answers our prayers because we force Him to, but He responds only out of His loving and free grace. It is a love that seeks to give more than we could ever possibly think to ask.

No prayer is ever wasted. God takes into account every prayer ever offered and is forever involved with us in charting the course of history. Even the prayers that we might have felt from our limited perspective went unheard had their answer in His own and perfect way. Every true prayer exposes the kingdom of Satan and helps establish the kingdom of God. Prayer presses back the forces of darkness. It battles back evil and error.

The more we pray, the more our horizons expand and the more we will come to expect from a supernatural, miracle-working God. But to ignore prayer leaves our life and outreach with only a secular or humanistic framework. We deny ourselves access to God's divine power and guidance in our lives. As God's last-day people, we must tap into His infinite power.

What Can Your Church Do to Grow Strong in Prayers?

1. A powerful church has leaders who make prayer a priority. If we take a careful look, we'll likely discover that our church's greatest deficiency is not in programs, strategies, materials, or ideas, but in prayer. Our church's greatest *strength* is prayer. Only prayer can release power for effective personal ministry. Prayer gives focus to the church's mission and enables us to fulfill that mission.
2. Prayer, Bible study, and personal ministry should be linked inseparably together. To do even prayer and Bible study without serving and sharing can create complacent, even self-centered Christians. All ministry without ample prayer preparation becomes only work in the

power of "the flesh." Whatever they might be, they are our attempts to do things in our human strength only.

Many are finding that one way to enhance their experience in prayer, Bible study, and ministry is to join a small group. Circles of friends meet regularly to pray, study, and then search out ways of helping others—in their homes, in their group, and in their communities. Both young people and adults are using this simple but life-changing method (see "Time-out and in Touch").

3. Make specific times, ways, and places to pray together—for church, for its leaders, and for the community. This encourages consistency in prayer. As we listen to others pray, hearing their experiences will strengthen our own prayer life. Praying together not only builds our faith, but makes the large task of prayer more manageable. We will not feel so overwhelmed, but will be encouraged. As many hands can carry the heaviest burdens, so many prayers can lift spiritual burdens.
4. Encourage personal and family devotions. Private prayer is the most spiritual, elevating activity that any soul can engage in. But one writer has said that if we neglect personal and family worship, "other attempts at prayer are like sprinkling the foliage of a plant with water while leaving the roots dry. God has chosen prayer as the key by which His church does its work. Through prayer we impact the world for God."

Time-out and in Touch

Here are some suggestions for small group prayer

and Bible study that will enrich the spiritual life and ministry of any church. Designed to provide a climate that will affirm, include, and make everyone free to participate, these suggestions, if followed, will create an atmosphere of warmth and fellowship as we bask in God's love and presence.

1. *First, provide an opportunity to get acquainted.* An "icebreaker" can be used, just a simple question such as "What is your favorite breakfast?" Limit this to five to 10 minutes. The icebreaker should involve something nonthreatening and brief.
2. *Second, everyone needs a Bible, notebook, and pen.* It will also be helpful to have *The Desire of Ages* or other resources available.
3. *The group must select a passage for study.* Gospel stories offer an excellent place to start. Some favorite passages are Luke 18:35-43 and 19:1-10.
4. *Give the simple guidelines to the group.* Remember that you want everyone to feel comfortable and to feel free to participate. It is better for group members to contribute at random rather than by "going around the circle." The facilitator leads but doesn't teach, and should speak less than the others. Acknowledge any and all contributions. The members of the group may ask any questions they wish—there are no poor questions or bad answers. Be sure to always maintain confidentiality. What the group discusses should never leave the group. Most important, keep the questions and comments related to the Scripture passage.
5. *Begin the group Bible study interaction with prayer.* The Holy Spirit will illumine hearts when we

allow Him into our lives. Invite the prayers of all who are interested in the success of the group.

6. *Read the passage through, with all participating, then take it verse by verse..* Encourage the group to ask questions about each verse (who, what, when, where, why, how). For example, who is involved in this story? Where are they? When? The context of the passage is important to understand what it is saying.
7. *Move freely into prayer as specific needs come up in the group.*
8. *Remain in the Scripture passage rather than taking side trips on personal stories or related issues.*
9. *After a discussion of the passage (for at least 30-40 minutes), the group should recap what it has discovered to this point.*
10. *Ask each other what new discoveries and thoughts have surfaced, getting several opinions.*
11. *After a summary of the thoughts and discoveries from the Scripture passage, pause for silent prayer.* During the silent prayer, each person should request the Holy Spirit's illumination again, this time for a specific and personal application from that Scripture study. Ask:
    - What does this mean to me personally?
    - What have I learned about Jesus?
    - What changes does He want to make in my life as a result of a deeper understanding of this passage or promise?
12. *Share personal applications in the group.*
13. *Close with prayer for the specific applications, needs, and requests that have surfaced.*
14. *Plan a time for ministry—individually and as a group.*

15. *Choose a passage for the next study and a new facilitator (optional).*
16. *Find a prayer partner in the group and pray daily for that person. At least once a week the partners should pray together.*

A Prayer Format

Jesus encouraged us to follow His approach in prayer, especially the Lord's Prayer. Here are some suggestions on how to do it. They follow key phrases in His prayer.

"Our Father in heaven."

This is the time for praise, because we are His children and He is a loving Father. Use texts of Scripture from the Psalms or other promises as we praise Him for all He is and does.

"Hallowed be Your name."

There are many ways to pray in this part of the prayer. Some people go through the days of Creation, citing examples of what God created on that day and praising God for His great power. Repeat scriptures with the many names of God or Hebrew names.

"Your kingdom come. Your will be done on earth as it is in heaven."

Pray for ourselves, our desire for the Holy Spirit, and our usefulness for God, then pray for others. Ask the Lord to show us whom to pray for. Besides praying for our family, pray for our pastors, teachers, and church leaders. Also, pray for the needs of our community.

"Give us this day our daily bread."

After finding the many promises of Scripture and

reminding God of His words, pray for spiritual, physical, emotional, professional, and financial needs.

"Forgive us our debts, as we forgive our debtors."

Ask the Lord to reveal to us the things in our life that He would like to change. Allow Him to show us our sins and to give us a hatred for those sins. Then we need to accept forgiveness and thank Him for it. Finally, we must ask Him for His grace to forgive others who have wronged us.

"Do not lead us into temptation, but deliver us from the evil one."

Ask Him to cover us with the whole armor of God, to spread the robes of the righteousness of Christ over us.

"For Yours is the kingdom and the power and the glory forever. Amen" (Matt. 6:9-13).

HOW TO FAST

Prayer and Fasting

The prayers of God's people have made almost unbelievable power available to us. Prayer and faith are our connection with God, who can do anything. All through Scripture God has worked in miraculous ways to rescue His children and to answer their prayers.

David, in Psalm 18:30, says that "the word of the Lord is proven true" and the message of Scripture from cover to cover is the same—we can trust His promises. Story after story gives us overwhelming evidence that He does rescue, He does deliver, He does provide, He does heal.

Peter and the disciples spent 10 days in prayer, just as Christ had instructed them to do. The result was

Pentecost and the outpouring of the Holy Spirit, which equipped them for service. Three thousand souls were converted that day, and it was just the beginning. The disciples themselves received boldness, courage, strength, and all the other abilities they needed.

Paul says in Romans 8:26 that we don't know what we want, or what we need, or what is required. But the Holy Spirit does. He intervenes and actually intercedes for us. Entering the presence of God, He discerns His mind and prays for us—not always according to our own prayers, but always according to the will of God.

The Holy Spirit may interrupt our prayers because we don't know how to pray as we should. Then He takes our feeble and stumbling prayers right into God's presence, where they are answered.

So often when we relate stories of miracles from Scripture or from more recent times, we focus on the exciting details of the miracle. Actually, if we go back to the very beginning of the biblical or other account, we see that the narrative begins with God's people on their faces before Him in prayer, and often there is not only prayer but also fasting. Then in answer to the united prayer and fasting of His people, God works His wonders, and His people come to realize more clearly who He is.

Adventists and Fasting

Adventists have used fasting in two ways: (1) to aid the body physically in *some* cases of disease and (2) in connection with prayer when they need special divine help. Since the focus of this book is on spiritual development, those interested in reading a collection of Ellen White's counsels regarding fasting as a *partial* remedy for *some* diseases should see *Counsels on Diet and Foods,* pages 189-191.

From the very earliest days of our movement, fasting has accompanied times of urgent prayer. During the Sabbath and sanctuary conferences of 1848 and 1849, when our pioneers were studying the basic doctrines of our fledgling church from the Bible, they sometimes spent entire days and nights in fasting and praying for light and guidance. In subsequent years, as urgent needs have arisen, the church has occasionally called upon members to join in a special day of fasting and prayer. Likewise, individual members, when facing a crisis of one nature or another, have utilized to good effect sessions of fasting and prayer while imploring God for wisdom and guidance.

Never, though, have Adventists entered fasting to earn any kind of merit with God. For anyone who might be tempted to think otherwise, Ellen White warned, "There are unbalanced minds that impose upon themselves fasting which the Scriptures do not teach, and prayers and privation of rest and sleep which God has never required. Such are not prospered and sustained in their voluntary acts of righteousness. They have a pharisaical religion which is not of Christ, but of themselves. They trust in their good works for salvation, vainly hoping to earn heaven by their meritorious works instead of relying, as every sinner should, upon the merits of a crucified, risen, and exalted Saviour" (*Testimonies for the Church,* vol. 1, pp. 556, 557).

No matter why we fast, we should never undertake it for show. Rather, fasting should always accompany genuine sorrow for sin and prayer for God's forgiveness. Ellen White has told us, "The fasting which the Word of God enjoins [in Matthew 6:16] is something more than a form. It does not consist merely in refusing food, in wearing sackcloth, in sprinkling ashes upon the head.

He who fasts in real sorrow for sin will never court display" *(Thoughts From the Mount of Blessing,* p. 87).

This may at least partially explain why Ellen White discouraged Adventists from long fasts, as some evangelical Christians are now undertaking. She wrote, "All the fasting in the world will not take the place of simple trust in the Word of God. 'Ask,' He says, 'and ye shall receive.' . . . You are not called upon to fast forty days. The Lord bore that fast for you in the wilderness of temptation. There would be no virtue in such a fast; but there is virtue in the blood of Christ" *(Counsels on Diet and Foods,* p. 189).

Despite these cautions against its possible misuse or abuse, fasting, as we will discover in the next section, when properly understood and utilized—and when accompanied by earnest prayer—can be a powerful experience for the Christian.

If we have decided to fast, we must ask ourselves, What is our objective? Is it spiritual renewal? guidance? healing? the resolution of problems?

Planning a Successful Fast

There are different kinds of fasts. Many people fast one day every week. During this time they drink only water. Others fast one meal a day, while still others abstain from heavy, rich foods and instead eat simple foods and lighter meals for a period of time. Another component of fasting is to eliminate secular influences such as reading, radio, and television.

If interested or impressed by the thought of fasting, we should first pray for guidance and direction. Should I fast? we ask ourselves. If so, *what kind* of fast should I undertake?

A vital element in fasting is that we devote extra

time to prayer. During the time we would usually have our meal we might try praying while walking with a friend or alone. By devoting the time to Bible study and prayer, we build spiritual muscles. And we may expect increased spiritual strength.

The Need to Fast

Why does Scripture emphasize the value of fasting? What can fasting mean in enhancing time in prayer?

When we pray, we take hold of the invisible. And when we fast, we let go of the visible. The writings of both Scripture and Ellen White offer the following biblical insights into the spiritual need for fasting:

1. Fasting enables us to gain humility and perspective in our lives. "I humbled myself with fasting" (Ps. 35:13). "Then I proclaimed a fast there at the river of Ahava, that we might humble ourselves before our God" (Ezra 8:21). "For certain things, fasting and prayer are recommended and appropriate. In the hand of God they are a means of cleansing the heart and promoting a receptive frame of mind. We obtain answers to our prayers because we humble our souls before God" *(Medical Ministry,* p. 283).
2. Fasting provides more time to pray, to seek God's presence, and to repent, because we are more focused on the Lord and less concerned with daily activities such as the preparation of meals and eating—things that center more on self.
3. The Holy Spirit uses fasting to reveal our true spiritual condition, leading to that brokenness, repentance, and character change that allows Him to work in an unusual and powerful way.

4. Fasting helps us to have clearness of thought and the ability to concentrate on the Word of God, to make it more meaningful, vital, and practical in our lives. Ellen White, in explaining the pioneers' group Bible studies, wrote: "One point at a time was made the subject of investigation. Solemnity characterized these councils of investigation. The Scriptures were opened with a sense of awe. Often we fasted, that we might be better fitted to understand the truth" *(Review and Herald,* July 26, 1892).
5. Fasting transforms prayer into a richer, deeper, and more personal experience. "It is in the order of God that those who bear responsibilities should often meet together to counsel with one another, and to pray earnestly for that wisdom which He alone can impart. Talk less; much precious time is lost in talk that brings no light. Let brethren unite in fasting and prayer for the wisdom that God has promised to supply liberally" *(Gospel Workers,* p. 417).
6. Fasting can help us regain a strong sense of spiritual determination and restore a deeper love for the Lord. "Now and onward till the close of time the people of God should be more earnest, more wide-awake, not trusting in their own wisdom, but in the wisdom of their Leader. They should set aside days for fasting and prayer. Entire abstinence from food may not be required, but they should eat sparingly of the most simple food" *(Counsels on Diet and Foods,* p. 188).
7. Fasting can build our faith and perseverance, enabling us to determine to stand on His Word.

Fasting Helps in a Number of Ways

1. Fasting is a primary means of restoration. Humbling ourselves by fasting opens the way for the Holy Spirit to do His special work of revival in us. This changes our relationship with God and gives us a greater awareness of His reality and presence in our lives.
2. Fasting reduces the power of self so that the Holy Spirit can do a more intense work within us.
3. Fasting brings an inner calm and self-control. It eliminates some of the physical distractions in our lives and leads to a slower pace and a more peaceful attitude. "The spirit of true fasting and prayer is the spirit which yields mind, heart, and will to God" (*Counsels on Diet and Foods,* p. 189).
4. Fasting renews spiritual vision. When we feel our life is out of control, or when we have lost our first love for the Lord, fasting can help us focus once again on God's plan for our lives. Fasting enables the Holy Spirit to draw us closer to Himself.
5. Fasting inspires determination to accept God's revealed plan for our life. Perhaps we know what God wants us to do but have a hard time following through with His plans. Fasting can help strengthen our resolve and keep us on track.
6. Fasting can help to bring revival.

Do You Really Want to Fast?

For all its spiritual benefits, fasting is not the easiest discipline to practice. For those unaccustomed to it, fasting can be a struggle. But it is well worth the effort. Scripture declares fasting and prayer to be a powerful means for allowing the fire of God to ignite again in a person's life. This fire produces the fruit of the Spirit—love, joy, peace, patience, kindness, goodness, faithfulness, gentleness, and self-control. Most important, the Holy Spirit will bring us the fruits of righteousness and the spiritual power to resist the lusts of the flesh and the lies of Satan.

As fasting and prayer bring surrender of body, soul, and spirit to our Lord and Saviour Jesus Christ, they also generate a heightened sense of the presence of the Holy Spirit. It creates a fresh, clean joy and a restored determination to serve God.

In His sermon on the mount, Jesus taught "*When* you fast," not "*If* you fast." For believers, then, the question is not *Should I fast?* but *When shall I fast?*

Adventist Christians around the world can fast for the sake of their homes, churches, and cities while personally experiencing the tremendous benefits of spiritual growth and increased peace and faith.

Fasting From Distractions

Fasting includes more than abstaining from food. It can include taking breaks from the noise and distraction of everyday life. We can turn off the TV and stereo, put away secular books and magazines, and take time off from ordinary duties and use the time for spiritual matters. Here are some things you could do during such fasts from noise and confusion:

- Pray for God's will to be done in your life. Pray out loud! Take an evening walk.
- Talk to God about your family, friends, neighbors, and work.
- Play games with some kids, showing them the love and attention all young people need.
- Ride a city bus for the entire length of its route,

talking to its passengers on the way.

- Write special Bible promises on index cards and memorize them while you jog, bike, walk, or roller blade.
- Pray for people in countries such as Afghanistan, North Korea, and India, where millions of people need Christ.
- Plan a sunrise breakfast picnic in the park with friends.
- Sing your favorite Christian songs while driving.
- Go through your old photographs or yearbooks and pray for your friends in the pictures.
- Check out a pet from the Humane Society and take it visiting at a nursing home.
- Pray for people who are ministering to suffering people around the world. Pray for the orphans, the war-stricken, and the starving.
- Photocopy chapters from your Bible (e.g., Isa. 55; 1 Cor. 13; Rom. 8) and memorize them.
- Purchase a Bible translation you have always wanted and read the book of Acts.
- Find one person to pray with every day.
- Memorize all five stanzas of "A Mighty Fortress Is Our God."
- Buy five pounds of bananas and hand-deliver them to different people living on the street.
- Pray five times a day for the one-billion Muslims in the world.
- Tell someone about Jesus.
- Study a church doctrine you have never understood.
- Memorize a verse from the Psalms before every meal.
- Read *The Pilgrim's Progress,* by John Bunyan.

- Pray for the apathetic affluent.
- Write a letter to a friend you haven't talked to for a long time.
- Pray for people you see in stores or people you talk to on the phone.
- Hold a special Bible study and prayer service with your family and friends at home.
- Read the book *Early Writings,* by Ellen White.
- Pray for friends who pop into your mind during the middle of the day.
- Climb a tree and read the story of Zacchaeus (Luke 19).
- Send someone a postcard or e-mail telling them that you are praying for them.
- Organize a youth outreach program for your church.
- Make, bake, and take bread to someone.
- Take flowers to a stranger in the hospital.
- Ask an elderly person to tell you the funniest thing that ever happened to them.
- Give someone who is begging on the street some money and ask them to pray with you right then.
- Always listen to God.

THOUGHT QUESTIONS FOR

COVENANT TWO

How to Pray

Ask Yourself . . .

• What are the things that the success of prayer depends on? Identify at least three factors on which our prayers rely for effectiveness.

• We may feel at times that we don't want to pray or that our prayers are futile. What is the connection between an attitude of surrender to God and our desire to pray? How can we increase our level of confidence in our prayers?

• The familiar aphorism from Ellen White, "prayer is the opening of the heart to God as to a friend" (*Testimonies,* vol. 4, p. 533), suggests that God welcomes any contact we make with Him. How might a conscious decision to view God as our friend encourage us to meet with Him and speak to Him more often?

• Especially for youth: God accepts prayer from anyone at any place, at any time. Have we ever stopped praying because we did something wrong? Would God listen to a prayer from us immediately after we have sinned? What kind of prayer might be appropriate at that moment?

How to Fast

Ask Yourself . . .

• As this chapter suggests, fasting is not easy and is not necessarily a gift or discipline everyone can exercise. For those of us who can do it, how can we think of fasting as a gift to God?

• Is it possible that fasting might make us conscious of a lack of dietary discipline at other times? What should we do about dietary imbalance?

• It might seem good to us to make fasting a regular habit. What might we do or think to avoid letting it become a physical habit, empty of spiritual significance? What activities should accompany fasting?

- Especially for youth: Do we have a purpose for fasting? What do we wish to accomplish by doing it?

"I Will Joyfully Share With Others at Every Opportunity My Experience With Christ, the Changes His Love Has Brought to My Life, and the Hope He Gives for the Future"

HOW TO WITNESS

If we look through a hole the size of a dime toward almost any spot in the sky, astronomers estimate that there will be 1,500 galaxies there—all created by Jesus. He who made those stars and planets would have died for just our neighbor next door. And He did it with the desire that our neighbor would sit on the throne of the universe with Him (see Rev. 3:20). Knowing this, how can we not tell our neighbor about His sacrifice and invitation? How can we not witness about a loving Lord who offers us the same love for our neighbor as He has us. "Christ will impart to His messengers the same yearning love that He Himself has in seeking for the lost" (*Christ's Object Lessons,* p. 235).

How God Arranges Witnessing Opportunities

Because of Jesus' unfathomable love for our neighbors, He will arrange casual contacts that provide us with opportunities to witness. He will also provide the wisdom (see James 1:5) that we need to cooperate with the Holy Spirit in preparing that person for His imminent return. If witnessing is to be our top priority, it is vital that we have a transformed mind. "Let Christians put away all dissension and give themselves to God for the saving of the lost. Let them ask in faith for the promised blessing, and it will come" *(Testimonies,* vol. 8, p. 21).

With the coming of the Lord right upon us, it is surely time for us to refocus our minds from our spiritual needs to a willingness to give ourselves to God for the saving of the lost. It is time for us to shift from being mere spectators to participants, from keepers of the aquarium to bold fishers of men and women. Our church exists to reach every person possible with judgment-hour urgency. If we would maintain a daily relationship with Jesus, we must reach out to others for Him. As we claim the infilling of His Spirit, the promise is: "All the requisite talent, courage, perseverance, faith, and tact will come as [we] put on the armor" *(ibid.,* vol. 6, p. 333). "When church members put forth earnest efforts to advance the message, they will live in the joy of the Lord and will meet with success" *(ibid.,* vol. 7, p. 30).

We must believe that God can and will use every one of us to witness. He has employed the most unlikely persons. It was almost impossible to understand anything Willie Brinninger said. He did not have the gift of clear speech. Yet for a time he topped the literature evangelists' sales record in North America.

One pastor conducted door-to-door Bible study techniques for anyone "who could smile and walk." One woman in the seminar could walk but couldn't smile. For three months she faithfully accompanied the pastor to Bible studies every Monday afternoon. At times the pastor almost felt like telling her that she didn't have the gifts necessary to give Bible studies. However, after three years she was a full-time literature evangelist and had realized seven baptisms from her personal Bible studies.

Another individual once announced from the pulpit that "everyone who can read and write can give Bible studies." Afterward someone came to her and said, "I cannot read and write, but give me some of those study guides." The church member took them to her neighbors and said, "I cannot read this, and I cannot write the answers here. Will you do that for me?" Soon she had 11 baptisms.

We must not limit ourselves or our abilities. Witnessing is not hard. It is natural and easy. As Jesus did, we must mingle with people, desiring their good. Forming redemptive friendships, we minister to needs as they arise. As we do we will be surprised to discover that most often the greatest needs that others have are spiritual ones. God will guide us to all those around us who are looking for spiritual help if we daily give ourselves to Him for the saving of the lost. Let us pray, "Who today, Lord?" Then we may watch as He miraculously brings opportunities to us among our families, friends, work associates, and neighbors on the bus, the train, the plane, at the market, or wherever we are. God is able to turn any casual visit to questions about life, death, or the future. Watch for opportunities and pray for words to turn the conversation toward Jesus and how we received the answers we needed through His Word.

How to Share Bible Truth With Others

"His peace in the heart will shine forth in the countenance. It will give to the voice a persuasive power" *(The Ministry of Healing,* p. 512). When people notice the joy and peace we have, they will begin to trust us and will ask us questions about current issues in the news or how to deal with difficulties. Then we can open our Bibles and say, "I had a similar question [or experience], and this text [or promise] was a great help to me." When the person responds favorably, we mustn't stop there but take it a step further. Have the first guide of a Bible course, such as the Discover series, handy at all times. Bringing it out, we can say, "I found this so helpful in answering many of the basic questions of life. I would like to share it with you. Take it home, and tomorrow [or the nearest date] tell me how you like it." If they have enjoyed it, give the next guide and ask them to fill out the answer sheet. Say: "I'm also doing them, and perhaps we can compare our answers."

Thus will begin a series of Bible studies in which as our friendship grows, we can review and discuss the questions in the guide and share our experience with Jesus. At the same time we will endeavor to lead them to a decision in every lesson. This systematic type of witnessing is the most rewarding, as we build on the other person's understanding and lead him or her first into a relationship with Jesus and then step-by-step into the joys of obedience, baptism, church membership, and small group fellowship. Finally, with support and training, the person will share with us the joys of witnessing.

Another way to arrange systematic Bible studies is to go door-to-door with a survey or a study guide. "This house-to-house labor, searching for souls, hunting for the lost sheep, is the most essential work that can be done" *(Evangelism,* p. 431). One witnessing leader had the privilege of training a group that started 5,640 studies.

Before Doug joined the church, he told a person who

had come to witness to him, "You either get out that door or I will push you out that window." But God can turn around the worst-case scenarios. Recently Doug and his trainee left Discover Bible guides in 139 homes. Six weeks later 89 persons had reached lesson 10! Doug now says, "Some people say door-to-door work isn't what it used to be. Praise God, it isn't. It's never been better." With prayer and a simple, positive, precise approach, we find that most people accept the first Bible guide at the door.

Here is a list of other possible candidates for systematic Bible studies: church guests, friends of newly baptized persons, missing members, literature evangelism paid-out accounts, Community Services patrons, and interest lists from Adventist magazines. People exposed to such Adventist media as *Amazing Facts, Voice of Prophecy, It Is Written, Breath of Life, Faith for Today,* 3ABN, and *Signs of the Times, Message, Liberty,* and *Vibrant Life* magazines provide other possible contacts. Also, non-SDA spouses, former seminar and evangelistic meeting attendees, church school non-SDA parents, Vacation Bible School parents, and SDA doctors' patients make good potential interests.

Success Secrets for Forming Friendships

Here are some secrets for gaining the confidence of individuals and forming productive, redemptive friendships. "Your success will not depend so much upon your knowledge and accomplishments, as upon your ability to find your way to the heart" *(Gospel Workers,* p. 193). "Our Saviour's power was not in a strong array of sharp words that would pierce through the very soul; it was His gentleness and His plain, unassuming manners that made Him a conqueror of hearts" *(Testimonies,* vol. 3, p. 477). "Satan is constantly seeking to produce effects by rude and violent thrusts; but Jesus found access to minds by the pathway of their most familiar associations. He disturbed as little as possible their accustomed train of thought" *(Evangelism,* p. 140).

We should pray continually for the love and tact Jesus showed to others. "Jesus did not suppress one word of truth, but He uttered it always in love" *(Steps to Christ,* p. 12). "In every human being He discerned infinite possibilities" *(Education,* p. 80). In addition, we may give special attention to His methods of witnessing as outlined in *The Desire of Ages*. As we become intensely interested in the other person, we can honestly say, "You are special. God has a plan for your life." People will respond to that.

"The tones of the voice have much to do in affecting the hearts of those that hear" *(Testimonies,* vol. 2, p. 615). We must not be cross or intentionally ruffle people's feathers. Nor must we condemn or argue. Although we may win the argument, we may lose the soul. Even if the person is argumentative, we must not oppose him or her or get pushy. "Christ saves none against their choice" *(ibid.,* vol. 3, p. 457). "Honor all people" (1 Peter 2:17). Accepting people where they are in their lifestyle and understanding will allow us to move them gently from their personal little island to where God wants them. Only the Holy Spirit knows exactly where people are on their heavenward journey. But we can get an idea if we will carefully listen to what they tell us.

Consider, for example, if we had just arranged to give a series of Bible studies to someone of whom we had no knowledge of his or her understanding or interests. What if when we knocked on the door to give the first study, the person met us with "Do you believe in speaking in tongues?" How should we respond?

The person to whom this actually happened didn't know what the woman believed and did not want to build a wall between them. Praying for wisdom, she threw the question back: "What do *you* believe about that?" "I believe it's of the devil," the woman replied. What if the person witnessing had not listened to the woman first before stating her own belief? Isn't it better to listen first and then build on the person's understanding?

During our initial visit we must always listen intently to whatever a person shares. At ease and relaxed, we will then ask inoffensive questions, such as inquiries about the person's family or occupation. Then when the individual is comfortable we can invite that person to share something about his or her religious background. If the individual is receptive, we can share our own testimony. We must not preach, but give a simple witness of our relationship with Jesus, tailoring it to the needs the person has expressed. This will help the person like both us and Jesus.

As we give a study we must put ourselves on the student's level. "Let us see what we can learn together," we can say. Complimenting the person in every way possible, we will agree on every point we can, while ignoring any error presented until we have covered that subject. Until then, we can say, "I understand how you feel." As we move at the student's pace, we will ask often whether a point is clear and will then use simple illustrations to help get it across. By constantly listening and watching the eyes and body language we can learn much about a person. If we keep the study quick and interesting, we will avoid boring the person.

God Will Use You

Many people think of Seventh-day Adventists as

the long-faced people who "can't do" and "don't do." But a daily relationship with Jesus will impel us to tell others what great things He has done for us, not what we can't do. As we do so we will witness about Jesus, proclaiming and demonstrating His goodness, love, justice, forgiveness, and victory. We will reflect the peace and assurance that He provides. Our first aim is not to convince people that we have the truth, but to awaken a heart response and commitment to a living personal Saviour, who is the answer to all their needs. Our 27 points of faith are important only as we know Jesus as a friend and accept Him as both Saviour and Lord. We must depict Christ as the center of every doctrine. But to do that, we ourselves need to know Jesus intimately and remain daily in a constant "vine-to-branch" union with Him. Witnessing thus becomes the best nurture there is as well as fulfilling the gospel commission.

Many Bible study guides have this vital focus. They lead the student to a decision for Jesus as Saviour and Lord, and then gently, unobtrusively, help build obedience into that relationship.

In all our witness, we must depend constantly on the Holy Spirit (see *Testimonies,* vol. 8, p. 21) and on prayer (see *The Desire of Ages,* p. 362). Then expect success, for we will have it (see *Welfare Ministry,* p. 101; *Testimonies,* vol. 6, p. 333; vol. 7, p. 30). God can use every one of us, whether we are young or old, rich or poor, highly educated or not.

HOW TO RESPOND TO GOD WITH ALL THAT I HAVE

When we realize God's greatness, His awesome power, and His wonderful plan of salvation, we naturally respond as King David did nearly 3,000 years ago: "What shall I render to the Lord for all His benefits toward me?" (Ps. 116:12). He then answered his own question by adding: "I will take up the cup of salvation, and call upon the name of the Lord. I will pay my vows to the Lord now in the presence of all His people" (verses 13, 14). We can never repay the Lord for all His blessings to us, but we can respond, as David did, by being faithful in our stewardship relationship with Him. God has outlined a simple plan that is a tangible, visible part of our covenant relationship with Him.

This covenant relationship between God and humanity rests on mutual promises: "He who gave His only-begotten Son to die for you has made a covenant with you. He gives you His blessings, and in return He requires you to bring Him your tithes and offerings" (*Counsels on Stewardship,* p. 75). Faithfulness in our stewardship, then, is a sign of our continuing covenant relationship with God.

To better understand our relationship to God we need to look at several biblical models:

God is the shepherd—we are the sheep.

God is our Father—we are His children.

God is eternal—we are like vapor.

God is the Creator—we are His creatures.

And in our stewardship relation:

God is the master—we are His stewards.

The true God is distinguished from all others by the fact that He is the Creator. And as Creator He is the owner of everything. We are simply His managers. "The earth is the Lord's, and all its fullness, the world and those who dwell therein" (Ps. 24:1). "If I were hungry, I would not tell you; for the world is Mine, and all its fullness" (Ps. 50:12). "That which lies at the foundation of business integrity and of true success is the recognition of God's ownership. The Creator of all things, He is the original proprietor. We are His stewards. All that we have is a trust from Him, to be used according to His direction" *(Education,* p. 137).

Stewardship Is More Than Money

"We are God's stewards, entrusted by Him with time and opportunities, abilities and possessions, and the blessings of the earth and its resources. We are responsible to Him for their proper use. We acknowledge God's ownership by faithful service to Him and our fellowmen, and by returning tithes and giving offerings for the proclamation of His gospel and the support and growth of His church. Stewardship is a privilege given to us by God for nurture in love and the victory over selfishness and covetousness. The steward rejoices in the blessings that come to others as a result of his faithfulness" (Fundamental Belief No. 20).

Living a Christian life means surrender—a giving up of ourselves and an accepting of Christ and His way. When we give all that we are and have to God, to whom it belongs anyway, He accepts it; but then puts us back in charge of it, making us stewards, or caretakers, of everything that we possess.

Stewards of Time

We say time flies. By that we mean that it seems to pass so quickly that we are not able to use it as effectively as we wish we could. Most people are so busy today that they have very little, if any, "free time." Even when they are away from the job they are still on duty by way of beepers, cell phones, fax machines, and e-mail. Our schedules are so busy that it is quite stressful just to keep up. Yet in the midst of our hectic lifestyles God says, "Be still, and know that I am God" (Ps. 46:10). The Sabbath, like the tithe, is holy, and giving it to God is an acknowledgment of His position as the great Creator-God.

God says, "Remember the Sabbath day, to keep it holy. Six days you shall labor and do all your work, but the seventh day is the Sabbath of the Lord your God. In it you shall do no work" (Ex. 20:8-10). In setting aside the Sabbath as holy time we honor God as Creator and let Him know that we are resting in Him. Non-Sabbath time, then, that we set aside for God and others is somewhat comparable to the offerings that we give to God in addition to the tithe.

Stewards of Talents

In addition to our time, each of us has talents, gifts, and abilities. God has blessed us with these assets so that we can provide for ourselves and help to advance His cause. When we exercise our stewardship responsibility in this area of our lives by using our gifts to bless others, we bring honor and glory to His name: "Whether you eat or drink, or whatever you do, do all to the glory of God" (1 Cor. 10:31). As Christians, one of our major concerns should be "How can I use the talents God has given me in the most effective manner in the upbuilding of His kingdom?"

Stewardship of Our Body Temple

Healthful living is simply the stewardship of our bodies, which we acknowledge as the temple of the Holy Spirit. It is not a matter of "works" that we choose a vegetarian lifestyle or attempt to maintain our ideal weight. Instead, we thank God for the timely scientific and practical counsel He has given us that contributes to our health and happiness. When properly understood, it is a joyful experience to practice healthful living. An understanding of the laws of health allows us to benefit from that "abundant life" that He came to secure for us.

God has claims upon us not only because of His position as Creator but also because He is our Redeemer. "Do you not know that your body is the temple of the Holy Spirit who is in you, whom you have from God, and you are not your own? For you were bought at a price; therefore glorify God in your body and in your spirit, which are God's" (1 Cor. 6:19, 20).

As Christian stewards we have the privilege of developing our physical and mental powers to the best of our ability and opportunities. In doing so, we bring honor to God and prove a greater blessing to our fellow humans.

Stewards of Our Environment

Many Christians are beginning to realize their stewardship responsibility for the earth—our environment. Because a majority of earth's inhabitants have failed to realize this, we now face serious and almost out-of-control environmental problems today. The combined resources of our church would not be sufficient to reverse the pollution of our planet. But we can do our part by not littering, not smoking, and keeping our yards and homes attractive as well as our churches and church schools. "Then God said, 'Let Us make man in Our image, according to Our likeness; let them have dominion . . . over all the earth'" (Gen. 1:26). What we do in this world is practice for the earth made new.

Apparently, God classified those who harm the earth as among the sinners who are destroyed at the end of the judgment. The 24 elders in heaven worship God and say, "The nations were angry, and Your wrath has come, and the time of the dead, that they should be judged, and that You should reward Your servants the prophets and the saints, and those who fear Your name, small and great, and should destroy those who destroy the earth" (Rev. 11:18).

Stewardship of the Truth

Perhaps the most misunderstood and yet most important area of stewardship is that of our stewardship of the truth. The Bible plainly tells us that we are "servants of Christ and stewards of the mysteries of God. Moreover it is required in stewards that one be found faithful" (1 Cor. 4:1, 2). Thus we must share what we know about God. As stewards of the truth, we are responsible for the good news about the great plan of salvation. We can exercise our stewardship individually by sharing our testimony. And we can do it collectively as a church family by working together to advance God's cause.

"Go therefore and make disciples of all the nations, baptizing them in the name of the Father and of the Son and of the Holy Spirit, teaching them to observe all things that I have commanded you; and lo, I am with you always, even to the end of the age" (Matt. 28:19, 20).

Stewardship of Our Treasure

Most of us, as we consider stewardship, think first and only about money. But as we have discussed above, stewardship and commitment to God involve all of life. However, the use we make of the money and other items of value that we possess is perhaps the greatest indication of our true relationship to God. It is also one of the most visible aspects of stewardship.

From the ancient records of Scripture we have reports of faithful tithing by Abraham (Gen. 14:20) and Jacob (Gen. 28:22). Apparently, ever since humanity's fall, God has used the tithing system as a test of allegiance. "The Lord placed our first parents in the Garden of Eden, He surrounded them with everything that could minister to their happiness, and He bade them acknowledge Him as the possessor of all things. In the garden He caused to grow every tree that was pleasant to the eye or good for food; but among them He made one reserve. Of all else, Adam and Eve might freely eat; but of this one tree God said, 'Thou shalt not eat of it.' Here was the test of their gratitude and loyalty to God.

"So the Lord has imparted to us heaven's richest treasure in giving us Jesus. With Him He has given us all things richly to enjoy. The productions of the earth, the bountiful harvests, the treasures of gold and silver, are His gifts. Houses and lands, food and clothing, He has placed in the possession of men. He asks us to acknowledge Him as the Giver of all things; and for this reason He says, Of all your possessions I reserve a tenth for Myself, besides gifts and offerings, which are to be brought into My storehouse. This is the provision God has made for carrying forward the work of the gospel" *(Counsels on Stewardship,* p. 65). The true motivation for tithing is to return to the Lord His portion of the blessings we receive. In other words, we don't tithe to get blessings. We give Him the tithe of the blessings He has already given us!

A Faithful Tithe—The Three P's

In order to be faithful and honest with God, we should consider three factors, all beginning with the letter P. The first P is for portion—the amount of the tithe. The Bible uses tithe and tenth interchangeably. For example, Abraham and Jacob gave a tenth. The portion, then, is 10 percent of our income if we are employees, or 10 percent of our increase or profits if we are in business for ourselves.

The second P is for place. Since the tithe is the

Lord's and is holy (Lev. 27:30), we must place it where He asks us to. He asks us to "bring all the tithes into the storehouse" (Mal. 3:10). In Bible times the storehouse was a room in the Temple—the treasury from which the priests paid the Levites. Down through time there have always been some who want to improve on God's plan and use their own discretion with regard to God's tithe. God told the Israelites, through Moses, "But you shall seek the place where the Lord your God chooses, out of all your tribes, to put His name for His habitation; and there you shall go. There you shall take your burnt offerings, your sacrifices, your tithes. . . . You shall not at all do as we are doing here today—every man doing whatever is right in his own eyes. . . . Take heed to yourself that you do not offer your burnt offerings in every place that you see; but in the place which the Lord chooses . . . there you shall do all that I command you" (Deut. 12:5-14).

Our church has established the conference office as the storehouse from which the pastors receive their pay. For convenience, we return the tithe at the local church, and the local treasurer sends it on to the conference storehouse.

The third P is for purpose. Since the tithe is the Lord's, it is not an offering. Therefore, the use we make of the tithe is not to be according to our discretion, but by God's direction. God said, "For the tithes of the children of Israel, which they offer up as a heave offering to the Lord, I have given to the Levites as an inheritance" (Num. 18:24). Since the Levites were full-time workers for Him, God used His tithe to support them.

Biblical Model

The Adventist Church has chosen to follow the biblical model today. "The tithe is the Lord's, and those who meddle with it will be punished with the loss of their heavenly treasure unless they repent. Let the work no longer be hedged up because the tithe has been diverted into various channels other than the one to which the Lord has said it should go. Provision is to be made for these other lines of work. They are to be sustained, but not from the tithe. God has not changed; the tithe is still to be used for the support of the ministry" *(Testimonies,* vol. 9, pp. 249, 250).

Offerings are the "frosting" of our financial stewardship. God has told us to bring offerings as He has prospered us. He has not set a fixed percentage of income that determines the amount of our offerings. They are based simply on our free will. The church may suggest percentages, but the choice is between us and the Lord. We also have discretion in the use of our offerings—what projects we support. Stewardship keeps us focused on our ultimate goal in life—spending eternity with Jesus. "For what will it profit a man if he gains the whole world, and loses his own soul? Or what will a man give in exchange for his soul?" (Mark 8:36, 37).

Our responsibility as Christian stewards is to take what God has given us—time, talents, our body temples, the earth's abundance, the truth we know about God, and our possessions—and use them wisely, with the perspective of bringing profit to the kingdom of God.

THOUGHT QUESTIONS FOR

COVENANT THREE

{How to Witness section}

Ask Yourself . . .

- What are some ways I can stay current with a secular worldview and connected to my community without compromising my Christian values?
- Is the fruit of the Holy Spirit so clearly evident in my own life that others are likely to desire such an experience? If not, what specific steps can I take to ensure that I reflect Christlike characteristics on a more consistent basis?
- List some individuals (at home, school, work, neighborhood, community, etc.) who right now seem in need of hearing about Jesus' love and the hope He brings to their future? How might I meet these persons' needs in a way that is nonthreatening and friendship-building?
- Especially for youth: How can my high energy and creative ideas be used to witness for Jesus?

[How to Respond to God With All That I Have section]

Ask Yourself . . .

- Is my life generally characterized by simplicity and balance? What areas need improvement? How could making such lifestyle changes help me exercise greater stewardship over my various God-given resources?
- What might I be "hoarding" that God could use for His purposes and to His glory?
- Am I modeling for others (family members, classmates, new church members, etc.) an approach to giving and stewardship that is Christlike and worthy of emulating? What steps can I take right now to ensure

a more responsible and consistent approach to stewardship in all areas?

- Especially for youth: What talents and/or resources might God be calling me to share in a special way for Him?

COVENANT FOUR

"I Will Lovingly Serve Jesus Christ as My Lord and Saviour and by His Power Prepare My Life for His Soon Return"

HOW TO PREPARE FOR THE LAST-DAY DECEPTIONS BEFORE CHRIST'S COMING

Jesus said, "For false christs and false prophets will arise and show great signs and wonders, so as to deceive, if possible, even the elect" (Matt. 24:24). Ellen White predicted in the closing chapters of *The Great Controversy* that the final deceptions of Satan will closely resemble truth. She speaks of Satan's "masterpiece of deception" (p. 561) and "the strong, almost overmastering delusion" (p. 624). How do God's people prepare for these last-day deceptions?

Accept the Fact That the Deceptions Will Be Real and That They Are Coming

Satan is pleased when we attempt to rationalize or explain away the prophecies that unfold the extent of the final deceptions. If as God's people we ignore these predictions or do not accept them, we will not be ready for the final conflict, and Satan's lies will sweep us away. Our experience will be similar to those who reject the existence of Satan. They will have no protection against his deceptive devices, and therefore will be easy prey.

Only as we accept the reality of the great controversy will we be in a position to acknowledge the magnitude of these massive delusions, detect them as they appear, and explain to ourselves and others why they exist. To be forewarned and to accept these warnings are the first steps in our preparation to survive the most extensive and deceptive campaign that Satan has ever launched against God's people. He knows this is the end, so he will pull out all of the stops to destroy everyone he can.

Test Everything by the Bible

Like the famous bomb-sniffing dogs that we have come to know on the evening news, Scripture alone will detect where the danger lies. We must reject everything that does not ring true when compared with the Bible. The apostle Paul counseled the Christians in Thessalonica: "Stand fast and hold the traditions which you were taught, whether by word or our epistle" (2 Thess. 2:15). The principle that Paul establishes here is vital today. Stand fast by holding to everything the Bible teaches. But in order to do that, we must take the time to fasten the truths of the Bible in our minds. We cannot detect error, nor can the Holy Spirit alert us to deception, if we have not fortified our minds with truth before error and deception attack us. Give some thought to the following counsel and warning from Ellen White:

"So closely will the counterfeit resemble the true that it will be impossible to distinguish between them except by the Holy Scriptures. By their testimony every statement and every miracle must be tested. . . . None but those who have fortified the mind with the truths of the Bible will stand through the last great conflict" *(The Great Controversy,* pp. 593, 594).

"Only those who have been diligent students of the Scriptures and who have received the love of the truth will be shielded from the powerful delusion that takes the world captive. . . . To all the testing time will come" *(ibid.,* p. 625).

"All whose faith is not firmly established upon the Word of God will be deceived and overcome" *(ibid.,* p. 560).

"Satan well knows that all whom he can lead to neglect prayer and the searching of the Scriptures will be overcome by his attacks" *(ibid.,* p. 519).

A knowledge of the Bible will protect us against all of Satan's deceptions.

Know What Forms the Final Deceptions Will Take

Jesus prophesied in Matthew 24:24 that Satan's last-day deceptions will come through false christs and false prophets. He also said that such lies will be so masterful that they will, if possible, deceive even God's people. To Jesus' prophecy the apostles Paul and John add the following:

1. Satan will work through the lawless one "with all power, signs, and lying wonders" (2 Thess. 2:9).
2. Satan will also operate through "deceiving spirits and doctrines of demons, speaking lies in hypocrisy" (1 Tim. 4:1, 2).
3. Satan's forces will produce great signs. Imitating Elijah, they will bring fire down from heaven, deceiving the people of earth (Rev. 13:13, 14).
4. Demonic spirits will work through the unholy

trinity—the beast, the false prophet, and the dragon—and will perform such amazing signs that they will be able to lead the world's rulers and their people to the "battle of that great day of God Almighty" (Rev. 16:13, 14).

In view of the scriptural passages above, we would do well to consider the fact that "little by little [Satan] has prepared the way for his masterpiece of deception in the development of spiritualism. He has not yet reached the full accomplishment of his designs; but it will be reached in the last remnant of time" (*The Great Controversy,* p. 561).

These passages reveal an overall view of the ways in which Satan will work. He will prompt false teachers to present lies so cleverly put together that they would deceive even God's people if it were not for their knowledge of the Bible. He will create powerful signs and wonders. Through the unholy trinity demons will lead the world on to destruction. All of these means of deception will be a part of Satan's masterpiece—spiritualism. When Ellen White penned the words quoted above, the modern forms of spiritualism were in their infancy. Spiritualism will achieve its full power to deceive "in the last remnant of time." Because it will be the major vehicle through which Satan will work at the end of time, we must take a deeper look into what the deception involves.

Master Everything the Bible Teaches About Death

Bible statements about the human condition in death fall into three general categories:

1. Both the Old and the New Testaments teach that death is an unconscious condition symbolically compared to sleep. Look up the word

"sleep" in any concordance, and it will give you numerous references.

2. Death has no consciousness or mental activity. David declared that the dead do not praise God (Ps. 115:17).
3. The third category contains just a handful of passages that seem to support the erroneous teaching of the existence of an immortal soul. But remember, we must interpret them in light of the overwhelming biblical evidence that death is a condition of total unconsciousness.

In view of last-day deceptions, why is it so important to understand what the Bible says about death? "Through the two great errors, the immortality of the soul and Sunday sacredness, Satan will bring the people under his deceptions" *(The Great Controversy,* p. 588). Accepting this statement at face value, we see why it is abundantly clear that we must understand the state of the dead.

Don't Trust Your Senses

Ellen White explains why it is vital to know what the Bible teaches about death: "Many will be confronted by the spirits of devils personating beloved relatives or friends and declaring the most dangerous heresies. These visitants will appeal to our tenderest sympathies and will work miracles to sustain their pretensions. We must be prepared to withstand them with the Bible truth that the dead know not anything and that they who thus appear are the spirits of devils" *(The Great Controversy,* p. 560).

It surprises some when they first read this statement. Certainly God would not permit such a thing to happen to His people, and certainly Satan would consider it a waste of time and energy to pull such a deception on those who know the truth about death. But it will happen, and it has already done so.

A girl less than 2 years old died in Africa some years ago. The missionary parents grieved their loss. A few weeks after the funeral the husband left on a trip. While he was gone, his wife had the following experience. As she sat in a chair, working on some household chores, her daughter, clothed in the dress she had been buried in, walked through the closed mahogany door, crossed the room, climbed up into the mother's lap, put her arms around the mother's neck, and said, "I love you, Mommy. I am not really dead." This happened to a Seventh-day Adventist mother.

The mother's experience was exactly what God had told Ellen White would happen and is proof that we cannot trust our senses. She saw, heard, and touched the child. Without a positive knowledge of what the Bible teaches, the deception could have had terrible results. But notice that Ellen White also said that "the most dangerous heresies" may accompany such personations. The time is approaching when the people of God must stand on Bible truth even though it means denying everything their senses tell them.

Oppose Spiritualism

John's description of Satan's preparation for the battle of Armageddon (Rev. 16:13, 14) makes it clear that spiritualism will be Satan's trump card in leading the world into the battle of the "great day of God Almighty." Ellen White tells us that he is determined to unite professing Christians and people of the world "in one body and thus strengthen his cause by sweeping all into the ranks of spiritualism" *(The Great Controversy,* p. 588).

Spiritualism involves more than supposed communication with the dead. Through Ellen White God alerted us to the philosophies embraced by spiritualism: "Spiritualism teaches 'that man is the creature of progression; that it is his destiny from his birth to progress, even to eternity, toward the Godhead.' . . . 'Any just and perfect being is Christ'" *(ibid.,* p. 554).

Each of these ideas appears in our society today. Human beings as evolving creatures lies at the foundation of evolution. Progress toward the Godhead occurs in the Mormon Adam/God doctrine. And "any just and perfect being is Christ" is a popular teaching of the New Age movement and grows out of Hindu mysticism. All of these philosophies, including communication with the dead, make up spiritualism in its broadest sense.

God's instruction to His people is "Combat it." "Those who oppose the teachings of spiritualism are assailing, not men alone, but Satan and his angels. They have entered upon a contest against principalities and powers and wicked spirits in high places. . . . The people of God should be able to meet him [Satan], as did our Saviour, with the words: 'It is written'" *(ibid.,* p. 559).

Know the Deceptions That Will Come Through Spiritualism

Besides those we have already looked at, Ellen White gives additional examples of the kind of deceptions we face.

1. Demons will produce terrifying phenomena: "Fearful sights of a supernatural character will soon be revealed in the heavens, in token of the power of miracle-working demons" *(The Great Controversy,* p. 624). This statement calls to mind the predictions of signs in the heavens

made during supposed appearances of the virgin Mary. According to such Marian apparitions, these cosmic signs will indicate God's soon-coming chastisement of sinners.

2. Demons will support Sunday laws: "Communications from the spirits will declare that God has sent them to convince the rejecters of Sunday of their error, affirming that the laws of the land should be obeyed as the law of God" *(ibid.,* p. 591).
3. Demons will claim to be the apostles: "The apostles, as personated by these lying spirits, are made to contradict what they wrote at the dictation of the Holy Spirit when on earth. They deny the divine origin of the Bible, and thus tear away the foundation of the Christian's hope and put out the light that reveals the way to heaven. . . . And to take the place of the Word of God he [Satan] holds out spiritual manifestations" *(ibid.,* p. 557).
4. Demons will pretend to be the gods of modern pagan religions: "As we near the close of time, there will be greater and still greater external parade of heathen power; heathen deities will manifest their signal power, and will exhibit themselves before the cities of the world" *(Evangelism,* p. 705).
5. Then there will come the greatest deception of all: "As the crowning act in the great drama of deception, Satan himself will personate Christ. . . . In his assumed character of Christ, he claims to have changed the Sabbath to Sunday, and commands all to hallow the day which he has blessed. He declares that those who persist in keeping holy the

seventh day are blaspheming his name by refusing to listen to his angels sent to them with light and truth. This is the strong, almost overmastering delusion" *(The Great Controversy,* p. 624).

Stand Firm on Bible Truth While You Deny Your Senses

Satan will use every means possible to convince us that we are wrong. It is important to take advantage of the relative calm that we are enjoying now to fortify the mind with truth. When the flood of deceptions washes over us, one hard on the heels of another, each of us will have to stand alone. No one else will be able to make the decision for us as to what is truth and what is error. That will be our responsibility. "To *all* the testing time will come."

HOW TO PREPARE TO RECEIVE THE LATTER RAIN AS WE NEAR CHRIST'S COMING

In Revelation 18:1 a mighty angel with great authority descends from heaven, flooding the earth with his glory. It is a prophetic representation of the coming latter rain. As the preaching of the gospel opened under the mighty power of the Holy Spirit, so it will close. In fact, the latter rain will prove to be a greater manifestation of God's power than was the early rain received by the apostles. But such power does not come without conditions. As the apostles prepared themselves to receive the early rain, so as God's people today—to an even greater degree—we must get ready for the latter rain. How, then, do we prepare for this final manifestation of God's power? Here are some instructions given to God's last-day church.

Grow Under the Early Rain

The early, or former, rain came to the apostles on the day of Pentecost. It enabled them to preach the gospel of salvation powerfully throughout the Roman Empire. Each person who accepts Jesus as his or her personal Saviour today also receives the early rain in the spiritual experience of baptism. In Palestine the early rain moistened the soil for plowing, germinated the seed, and allowed it to grow. Receiving the early rain enables us to grow and develop spiritually. An important law of growth states that once a seed is planted, it must be watered. This is true in our spiritual lives, too.

If the Holy Spirit plants and waters the gospel seed, the seed will take root and grow. However, as with any natural plant, if the plant that grows from the gospel seed receives no water, it will wither and die. The Holy Spirit launches us on the Christian pathway. Peter told his hearers on the day of Pentecost, "Repent, and let every one of you be baptized in the name of Jesus Christ for the remission of sins; and you shall receive the gift of the Holy Spirit" (Acts 2:38). The Holy Spirit enables us to grow and brings us to full spiritual maturity. Such spiritual growth requires a fresh watering of the Spirit's power every day.

Ellen White puts it this way: "At no point in our experience can we dispense with the assistance of that which enables us to make the first start. The blessings received under the former rain are needful to us to the end. . . . By prayer and faith we are continually to seek more of the Spirit" *(Testimonies to Ministers,* pp. 507, 508).

This and other similar statements make it clear that the latter rain is the final step in the Christian's spiritual growth, just as the last showers of Palestine's rainy season bring the crops to harvest. If, however, there is no daily growth in preparation for the latter rain, the Christian will not be ready when the latter rain falls. For this reason, we are to pray daily for a fresh baptism of the Holy Spirit as we mature under the early rain.

God, in His wisdom, has given us the following caution: "We may be sure that when the Holy Spirit is poured out, those who did not receive and appreciate the early rain will not see or understand the value of the latter rain" *(Manuscript Releases,* vol. 1, p. 180).

Seek for the Spirit Now

The great danger we as God's people face today is procrastination. Yes, the latter rain is coming. Yes, we have the promises. But we tend to think that this experience will happen sometime in the distant future. Remember—and we cannot stress this enough—the falling of the latter rain will be the final step in the Christian's spiritual growth. Thinking the latter rain will come to everyone sometime *in the future* can only lead us to delay in preparing for it.

Ellen White presses upon our minds the urgency of getting ready today: "The descent of the Holy Spirit upon the church is looked forward to as in the future; but it is the privilege of the church to have it now. Seek for it, pray for it, believe for it. We must have it, and Heaven is waiting to bestow it" *(Evangelism,* p. 701). The urgency that she felt for immediate preparation appears in the three commands: "Seek . . . pray . . . believe."

Stand Firm When Tested

The presence of the Holy Spirit will bring dynamic power to the Christian life, as we see in the experience of the apostles. With words that cut to the hearts of their hearers, they boldly witnessed for Jesus in the face of threatened beatings and death. With the simple logic of truth they confounded those who opposed the gospel. God worked miracles through them. Because we can abuse such power by turning it to self-glorification, God first wants to see evidence that we will not misuse it. "Before giving us the baptism of the Holy Spirit [the latter rain], our heavenly Father will try us, to see if we can live without dishonoring Him" *(Selected Messages,* book 3, pp. 426, 427).

Although being sifted by God is unpleasant at times, it is for our own good. Remember that Jesus said to the Laodiceans, "As many as I love, I rebuke and chasten" (Rev. 3:19). We must, therefore, discipline ourselves to look upon God's chastenings as preparatory steps for being entrusted with the power that He will give His church in the latter-rain experience.

Imitate the Apostles

The experience of the apostles in preparing for Pentecost is a model that, if followed, will lead us to proper preparation for the latter rain. In fact, Ellen White directs us back to their experience to see what God requires of us. "It was by the confession and forsaking of sin, by earnest prayer and consecration of themselves to God, that the early disciples prepared for the outpouring of the Holy Spirit on the Day of Pentecost. The same work, only in greater degree, must be done now" *(Testimonies to Ministers,* p. 507).

The 10-day period between the ascension of Jesus and the day of Pentecost was a time of intense preparation on the part of the apostles. Luke alludes to it when he says: "These all continued with one accord in prayer and supplication, with the women and Mary the mother of Jesus, and with His brothers" (Acts 1:14). In her book *The Acts of the Apostles*, Ellen White offers greater detail: (1) the apostles met together and prayed frequently about the work that Jesus had given them to do on earth; (2) they humbled their hearts in true repentance and confessed their unbelief; (3) they had a deep desire to be clothed in the loveliness of His character as they thought of Jesus' holy life and shared their remembrances of Him; (4) they put away all differences, jealousy, and desires for supremacy, and drew together in Christian love and fellowship; (5) they prayed for wisdom to bring souls into Jesus' kingdom; and (6) they prayed specifically for the gift of the Holy Spirit in fulfillment of Jesus' promise (pp. 35-37). Here is a model that an individual or an entire congregation can follow.

Work at Fulfilling the Conditions

The great apostle of righteousness by faith told the Philippians: "Work out your own salvation with fear and trembling" (Phil. 2:12). At the time Paul did not explain in detail what that work was to be, but it is clear that all believers have a role to play in God's plan of salvation. And in receiving the promised power of the latter rain, we also have a part. Only in this case the work that we are to do is clearly defined: "Our heavenly Father is more willing to give His Holy Spirit to them that ask Him, than are earthly parents to give good gifts to their children. But it is our work, by confession, humiliation, repentance, and earnest prayer, to fulfill the conditions upon which God has promised to grant us His blessing" *(Selected Messages,* book 1, p. 121).

What could be clearer? Confession, humiliation, and repentance brought us to Christ, and we found His grace and were clothed in His righteousness. This experience is to deepen day by day as we grow in the early-rain experience. Paul says: "As you have therefore received Christ Jesus the Lord, so walk in Him" (Col. 2:6). Now we add fervent prayer for the promised gift of the latter rain. The prophet Zechariah instructs us: "Ask the Lord for rain in the time of the latter rain" (Zech. 10:1). The quest for the latter rain is to be as intense as the quest for life itself. As Jesus valued the promised Holy Spirit for His apostles, so He places a high value upon the power that will enable His people to fulfill the gospel commission today.

Get Ready Now, Because the Latter Rain Is Coming Suddenly

When God gives the latter rain, it will come suddenly, and everything will be over. It will be that quick! When the time arrives in the progression of the great controversy for the full display of God's power and glory, His people will not have an opportunity then to make the preparations that should be in progress today. It is become ready now or be left behind.

The early Adventist experience of the Midnight Cry hints at the rapidity and urgency with which the latter rain approaches. "I saw the latter rain was coming [as suddenly] as the midnight cry, and with ten times the power" *(Spalding and Magan Collection,* p. 4). The Midnight Cry appeared suddenly and quite unexpectedly at the Exeter, New Hampshire, camp meeting, August 12-17, 1844, when Samuel S. Snow explained to the assembled Millerites that the ancient Jewish rite of cleansing the sanctuary fell on October 22 that year. The Millerites left that meeting and scattered everywhere, proclaiming, "Behold, the Bridegroom cometh."

Ellen White describes the rapidity with which God will wind up the work on earth: "There will be an accumulation of divine agencies to combine with human effort that there may be the accomplishment of the work for the last time. The work will most assuredly be cut short in a most unexpected manner. . . . There will be thousands converted to the truth in a day, who at the eleventh hour see and acknowledge the truth and the movements of the Spirit of God. 'Behold, the days come, saith the Lord, that the plowman will overtake the reaper, and the treader of grapes him that soweth seed' (Amos 9:13).

"The accessions to the truth will be of a rapidity which will surprise the church" *(The Ellen G. White 1888 Materials,* pp. 754, 755).

The realization that the latter rain will happen suddenly and quite unexpectedly emphasizes the importance of the first section of this study. Unless we are growing day by day under the early rain, we will not be ready for the latter rain. For the latter rain is simply the concluding step in early-rain growth. Without that previous maturing, without the daily baptism of the Holy Spirit, we will not have adequate time to catch up to the point where God can trust us with the latter-rain power. For this reason, God seeks to inform all His people what must be done now so none need be left behind.

Jesus emphasized the importance and urgency of preparing for the gift that He valued so highly when He said: "Ask, and it will be given to you; seek, and you will find; knock, and it will be opened to you.' . . . If you then, being evil, know how to give good gifts to your children, how much more will your heavenly Father give the Holy Spirit to those who ask Him!" (Luke 11:9-13). With the assurance of this promise from Jesus Himself, we can press on with confidence to the final step in early-rain growth.

Without a doubt Jesus will be here soon. Signs of the end abound, and it is time for the latter rain. How often have we told one another, "When we see the formation of the image of the beast and a movement toward enforcing Sunday, we will surely know the end is upon us"? Protestantism is pressing hard for the development of a working relationship with Rome, and Rome has shown itself to be a willing partner. The pope's call to protect the sanctity of Sunday by civil legislation may well be the initial step toward the enforcement of the mark of the beast. By these and other signs, God is calling His people to renew their covenant relationship with Him. We are standing on the borders of the Promised Land—let us arise and go in.

THOUGHT QUESTIONS FOR

COVENANT FOUR

{How to Prepare for the Last-Day Deceptions Before Christ's Coming section}

Ask Yourself . . .

• What attitude, person(s), or circumstances might be keeping me from consistently opening myself to God's truth in its various forms (the Bible, Spirit of Prophecy writings, sermons, group study, publications, etc.)? How can this change?

• Am I outfitted daily with God's spiritual "armor," as mentioned in Ephesians 6:14-17 (truth, righteousness, gospel of peace, faith, the Word of God)?

• What changes might I need to make in my lifestyle that could help prepare me to discern truth from error more effectively?

• Especially for youth: What are some areas of youth culture that seem especially fertile for spiritual degeneration and deception? What specific choices have we made, or could we make, that would help protect us from such potential evil?

{How to Prepare to Receive the Latter Rain as We Near Christ's Coming}

Ask Yourself . . .

• What situation(s) in my life right now stands in need of repentance and confession? What steps will I take to put these matters to rest?

• Do I look forward to the latter rain and the end-time with joy, anticipation, and confidence, or does fear more accurately describe my feelings? If I am apprehensive about the end-time, what steps can I take to change this?

• What are some advantages of becoming involved in a small group whose goal is to prepare for the latter rain?

- Especially for youth: Am I "hardened" to the idea that "Jesus is coming soon"? If so, how might I capture a sense of expectancy regarding my Saviour's return while keeping a balanced view of the end?

WORDS OF ENCOURAGEMENT

Recently the editor of a major news magazine wrote an editorial decrying the fact that by many in the United States, Christianity and morality are looked down upon and even made fun of. In this time of rampant disregard for the principles and teachings of Scripture, as well as the lack of true spirituality, it is vitally important for Adventist Christians to be anchored in the Word and the Spirit of Prophecy. Only as we spend more time in study and fellowshipping with our precious Saviour in prayer will we be able to withstand the growing influences of the powers of darkness.

Malcolm and Hazel Gordon,
Southern Union Conference

In view of the imminent return of Jesus and the cataclysmic events that precede it, we are reminded of an insightful statement by Ellen White, "We have only to live one day at a time, and if we get acquainted with God, He will give us strength for what is coming tomorrow." *My Life Today,* p. 94. We want to join with you in getting better "acquainted with God" one day at a time.

Jere and Sue Patzer, North
Pacific Union Conference

The return of Jesus is a pleasant and happy thought for us. In preparation for His grand event we invite you to join us in the continued study of the Bible and Spirit of Prophecy. By so doing we will draw close to Him and be ready to join Him when He comes to get His chosen ones.

Max and Betty Trevino,
Southwestern Union
Conference

We are now living in the very exciting times when everything that can be challenged or shaken is experiencing those very actions. There is a feeling in the air of expectancy, and we know that soon Christ will return. More than ever before we need the power of God's Spirit in our lives, homes, and churches. Studying the Bible and the Spirit of Prophecy, praying earnestly and sharing the good news, is the need of every Adventist member. The times demand it! This will give us joys in abundance!

Ted and Esther Jones,
Atlantic Union Conference

It has been rightly said, "We are what we think." The only way to reflect God in our lives is by letting His words transform our minds until we become like Him in thought and action. Here is the path to spiritual revival. There is no substitute or shortcut.

Tom and Pauline Mostert,
Pacific Union Conference

Ever since the gospel of God's saving grace found us and made us a part of the Adventist community of faith, our hope has been on meeting the Lord Jesus. We are committed to Him in service and the study of His precious Word. We believe that earnest prayer and study of the Bible will bring the long-awaited promise of revival and reformation.

Harold and Barbara Lee,
Columbia Union Conference

Demanding schedules, overstacked mail trays, constant telephone calls, and e-mail messages seem to dominate our days. As we struggle to minister effectively, we are often pushed for time, making it easy to allow relationships to slip, especially the most important relationship of all—the one with Jesus. We are often overwhelmed with the need to stay closely connected with Him in prayer and Bible study as we become increasingly aware of the challenges before us. As we accept His invitation to lay all our anxieties on Him, we have discovered that He keeps His promise of giving us His peace and His strength to cope with the pressures we daily encounter and the uncertainties of these last days. Truly, our lifeline is staying in a daily intimate and meaningful relationship with Him through studying His Word and communing with Him in prayer. There is absolutely no substitute.

Orville and Norma Jean Parchment,
SDA Church in Canada

Knowing Jesus—this is the most important thing in this life! We have found from personal experience that the more we read of His messages to us, the closer we are to Him. And the closer we are to Him, the more excited we are about seeing Him again. Won't you join us in our commitment to spend time with Him each day?

Don and Marti Schneider,
Lake Union Conference

A promise that has great meaning to us now is this one found in 1 Chronicles 28 that says: "Be strong and of good courage; . . . do not fear nor be dismayed for the Lord God—my God, will be with you." He is with us because He is our Friend.

Chuck and Dona Sandefur
Mid-America Union Conference

APPENDIX A

The following sections are samples of what can be done for systematic Bible and Spirit of Prophecy reading. Feel free to develop your own schedule or use other alternatives for spiritual study.

"Study to show thyself approved unto God, a workman that needeth not to be ashamed, rightly dividing the word of truth" 2 Timothy 2:15.

"It is the duty of everyone to seek a thorough knowledge of the Scriptures. The importance and benefit of Bible study cannot be overestimated. In searching the Scriptures our minds are caused to dwell upon the infinite sacrifice of Christ, on His mediation in our behalf . . . As we behold Jesus by the eye of faith, we shall be 'changed into the same image from glory to glory, even as by the Spirit of the Lord'" (*Signs of the Times,* February 6, 1893).

BIBLE READING PLAN FOR ONE YEAR

Day	
1	Genesis 1:1-2:3
2	Genesis 2:4-25
3	Genesis 3
4	Genesis 4:1-16
5	Genesis 5:18-24; Jude 14, 15
6	Genesis 6
7	Genesis 7
8	Genesis 8:1-9:17
9	Genesis 11:1-9
10	Genesis 11:27-12:9
11	Genesis 12:10-20
12	Genesis 13
13	Genesis 14

Day	
14	Genesis 15
15	Genesis 16:1-16; 21:1-21
16	Genesis 18
17	Genesis 19:1-29
18	Genesis 20
19	Genesis 22:1-18
20	Genesis 23
21	Genesis 24
22	Genesis 25:19-34
23	Genesis 27
24	Genesis 28:10-22
25	Genesis 29:1-14
26	Genesis 29:15-30
27	Genesis 31:1-21

Day

28 . . . . Genesis 32
29 . . . . Genesis 33
30 . . . . Genesis 34
31 . . . . Genesis 35:1-15
32 . . . . Genesis 37
33 . . . . Genesis 39
34 . . . . Genesis 41
35 . . . . Genesis 42
36 . . . . Genesis 43
37 . . . . Genesis 44
38 . . . . Genesis 45
39 . . . . . . Genesis 46:1-47:12
40 . . . . Genesis 48; 49
41 . . . . Genesis 50
42 . . . . Job 1
43 . . . . Job 2
44 . . . . Job 29
45 . . . . Job 42
46 . . . . Exodus 1:1-2:10
47 . . . . Exodus 2:11-25; Psalm 90
48 . . . . Exodus 3:1-4:17
49 . . . . Exodus 4:18-6:8
50 . . . . Exodus 7:1-9:12

Day

51 . . . . Exodus 9:13-11:10
52 . . . . Exodus 12
53 . . . . . . Exodus 13:17-14:31
54 . . . . Exodus 16
55 . . . . Exodus 17
56 . . . . Exodus 19; 20
57 . . . . Exodus 32
58 . . . . Exodus 33:7-34:9
59 . . . . Exodus 40
60 . . . . Leviticus 10
61 . . . . Leviticus 11
62 . . . . Leviticus 16
63 . . . . Leviticus 23
64 . . . . Numbers 11

Day

65 . . . . Numbers 12
66 . . . . Numbers 13
67 . . . . Numbers 16
68 . . . . Numbers 17
69 . . . . Numbers 20:1-13
70 . . . . Numbers 20:22-21:9; 2 Kings 18:4
71 . . . . Numbers 22-24
72 . . . . Deuteronomy 6
73 . . . . Deuteronomy 8
74 . . . . Deuteronomy 26
75 . . . . Deuteronomy 28
76 . . . . Deuteronomy 30
77 . . . Deuteronomy 32:48-52; 34:1-12
78 . . . . Joshua 1
79 . . . . Joshua 2
80 . . . . Joshua 3
81 . . . . Joshua 5:13-6:27
82 . . . . Joshua 7
83 . . . . Joshua 9
84 . . . . Joshua 10:1-21
85 . . . . Joshua 14
86 . . . . Joshua 22
87 . . . . Joshua 23; 24
88 . . . . Judges 2
89 . . . . Judges 4
90 . . . . Judges 6
91 . . . . Judges 7
92 . . . . Judges 13
93 . . . . Judges 15
94 . . . . Judges 16
95 . . . . Ruth 1; 2
96 . . . . Ruth 3; 4
97 . . . . 1 Samuel 1
98 . . . . 1 Samuel 3
99 . . . . 1 Samuel 4

Day

100 . . . . 1 Samuel 5; 6

DAY

101 . . . . 1 Samuel 7
102 . . . . 1 Samuel 8
103 . . . . 1 Samuel 9:15-10:24
104 . . . . 1 Samuel 12
105 . . . . 1 Samuel 13:1-14
106 . . . . 1 Samuel 14:1-23
107 . . . . 1 Samuel 15
108 . . . . 1 Samuel 16
109 . . . . 1 Samuel 17
110 . . . . Psalm 37
111 . . . . 1 Samuel 18:1-9; 19:1-7; 20:1-17
112 . . . . 1 Samuel 21
113 . . . . Psalm 34
114 . . . . 1 Samuel 24
115 . . . . 1 Samuel 25
116 . . . . 1 Samuel 28
117 . . . . 1 Samuel 31
118 . . . 2 Samuel 2:1-7; 5:1-12
119 . . . . 2 Samuel 6
120 . . . . 2 Samuel 7
121 . . . . Psalm 18
122 . . . . 2 Samuel 9
123 . . . . 2 Samuel 11; 12
124 . . . . Psalm 32 or 38
125 . . . . Psalm 51
126 . . . . Psalm 103
127 . . . . 2 Samuel 15; 16
128 . . . . Psalm 55
129 . . . . . 2 Samuel 17:1-19:8
130 . . . . 2 Samuel 24
131 . . . . 1 Kings 1
132 . . . . Psalm 72
133 . . . . 2 Samuel 23:1-7; 1 Kings 2:1-12
134 . . . . . . 1 Kings 3; 4:29-34
135 . . . . Proverbs 3
136 . . . . 1 Kings 8
137 . . . . 1 Kings 10:1-13
138 . . . . Proverbs 23

DAY

139 . . . . 1 Kings 11
140 . . . . . . Proverbs 6:20-7:27
141 . . . . Ecclesiastes 11; 12:1, 9-14
142 . . . . 1 Kings 12
143 . . . . 1 Kings 14
144 . . . . . 1 Kings 16:29-17:6
145 . . . . 1 Kings 17:7-24
146 . . . . 1 Kings 18
147 . . . . 1 Kings 19
148 . . . . 1 Kings 20
149 . . . . Psalm 91
150 . . . . 1 Kings 21

DAY

151 . . . . 1 Kings 22:1-40
152 . . . . 2 Kings 2:1-18
153 . . . . 2 Kings 4:1-37
154 . . . . 2 Kings 2:19-22; 4:38-44
155 . . . . 2 Kings 5
156 . . . . 2 Kings 6:1-23
157 . . . . . . 2 Kings 6:24-7:20
158 . . . . 2 Kings 9
159 . . . . 2 Kings 11
160 . . . . 2 Kings 12
161 . . . . Jonah 1; 2
162 . . . . Jonah 3; 4
163 . . . . Amos 5
164 . . . . Hosea 1; 3
165 . . . . 2 Kings 17
166 . . . . 2 Chronicles 26
167 . . . . Micah 6:6-8; 7:8-11, 18-20
168 . . . . Isaiah 6
169 . . . . Isaiah 24
170 . . . . 2 Kings 18:1-16
171 . . . . 2 Kings 18:17-19:13
172 . . . . 2 Kings 19:14-37
173 . . . . 2 Kings 20

DAY

174 . . . . Isaiah 42
175 . . . . . . Isaiah 52:13-53:12
176 . . . . Isaiah 54
177 . . . . Isaiah 58
178. . . . . 2 Kings 21:1-18
179 . . . . 2 Chronicles 34:8-28
180. . . . . Joel 2
181 . . . . . . Habakkuk 1:1-2:4
182. . . . . Habakkuk 3
183 . . . . Jeremiah 1
184. . . . . . Jeremiah 17:19-27; Nehemiah 13:15-22
185 . . . . Jeremiah 18:1-17
186 . . . . Jeremiah 36
187 . . . . Jeremiah 37; 38
188 . . . . Ezekiel 1
189 . . . . Ezekiel 8; 9
190 . . . 2 Chronicles 36:11-21 or Jeremiah 52
191. . . . . Lamentations 3:1-41
192. . . . . Psalm 74 or 79
193 . . . . Psalm 137
194. . . . . Daniel 1
195. . . . . Daniel 2
196. . . . . Daniel 3
197. . . . . Daniel 4
198. . . . . Daniel 5
199. . . . . Daniel 6
200. . . . . Daniel 7

DAY

201 . . . . Jeremiah 51
202 . . . . Ezra 1
203 . . . . Haggai 1; 2
204 . . . . Zechariah 3; 4
205 . . . . Ezra 5; 6
206. . . . . Nehemiah 1; 2
207 . . . . Nehemiah 5
208 . . . . Nehemiah 8
209 . . . . Esther 2:1-18

DAY

210. . . . . Esther 3
211. . . . . Esther 4
212. . . . . Esther 7; 8
213. . . . . Malachi 3:6-17
214 . . . . Luke 1:5-25
215 . . . . . . Matthew 1:18-25; Luke 2:1-7
216. . . . . Luke 2:8-20
217 . . . . Luke 2:21-40
218 . . . . Matthew 2:1-12
219 . . . . Matthew 2:13-23
220 . . . . Luke 2:41-52
221 . . . . John 1:19-34
222 . . . . Matthew 4:1-11
223 . . . . . . Matthew 4:23-25; Luke 4:14-30
224 . . . . John 2:1-11
225 . . . . John 2:13-25
226 . . . . John 3:1-21
227 . . . . John 3:22-36
228 . . . . Matthew 14
229 . . . . John 4:1-42
230 . . . . John 4:43-54
231 . . . . Luke 5:1-11
232 . . . . John 5
233 . . . . Matthew 5
234 . . . . Matthew 6:5-15
235 . . . . Matthew 6:19-34
236 . . . . Luke 4:16-30
237. . . . . Mark 1:21-39
238 . . . . Luke 5:12-26
239 . . . . Matthew 10
240 . . . . Mark 2:23-3:6
241 . . . . Luke 7:1-10
242 . . . . Luke 7:11-17
243 . . . . Matthew 8:18-27
244. . . . . Mark 5:1-20
245 . . . . Matthew 9:18-26
246. . . . . Mark 4:26-34
247 . . Matthew 13:1-9, 18-23

DAY

248 . . . . . . Matthew 21:33-45
249 . . . . Matthew 22:1-14
250 . . . . Luke 14:15-24

DAY

251 . . . . . . Matthew 18:21-35
252 . . . . Luke 15:1-10
253 . . . . Luke 15:11-32
254 . . . . Matthew 20:1-16
255 . . . . Luke 10:25-37
256 . . . . Matthew 7:24-28
257 . . . . Luke 5:27-35
258 . . . . Matthew 14:1-12
259 . . . . John 6:1-15
260 . . . . Matthew 17:1-13
261 . . . . Mark 9:14-29
262 . . . . John 8:2-11
263 . . . . . . Matthew 17:24-27
264 . . . . John 9:1-25
265 . . . . John 10:1-21
266 . . . . Luke 7:36-50
267 . . . . Luke 10:38-42
268 . . . . John 11:17-44
269 . . . . Luke 17:11-19
270 . . . . Luke 18:9-14
271 . . . . . . Matthew 19:16-30
272 . . . . . . Matthew 20:20-28
273 . . . . Luke 19:1-10
274 . . . . Luke 19:11-27
275 . . . . Matthew 21:1-11
276 . . . . . . Matthew 22:15-45
277 . . Matthew 26:1-5, 14-16
278. . . . . Mark 12:38-44
279 . . . . Luke 13:34, 35;
John 12:37-50
280 . . . . Matthew 24
281 . . . . Matthew 25:1-13
282 . . . . Luke 22:7-23
283 . . . . John 14
284 . . . . John 15:1-17

DAY

285 . . . . John 17
286 . . . . . . Matthew 26:36-56
287 . . . . John 18:12-24
288 . . . . . . Matthew 26:57-75
289 . . . . Matthew 27:1-10
290 . . . . Luke 23:1-12
291 . . . . Luke 23:8-25
292 . . . . Luke 23:26-56
293 . . . . . . Matthew 28:1-15;
John 20:1-18
294 . . . . Luke 24:13-35
295 . . . . Luke 23:36-49
296 . . . . John 21:1-14
297. . . . . Luke 24:44-52;
Acts 1:1-11
298 . . . . Acts 2:1-24
299 . . . . Acts 3
300 . . . . Acts 4:1-22

DAY

301 . . . . Acts 4:32-5:11
302 . . . . Acts 6:1-7
303 . . . . Acts 6:8-15; 7:51-8:2
304 . . . . Acts 8:9-25
305 . . . . Acts 8:26-40
306 . . . . Acts 9:1-31
307 . . . . Acts 9:36-43
308 . . . . Acts 10:1-48
309 . . . . Acts 12:1-19
310 . . . . Acts 13
311 . . . . Acts 15:36-40;
2 Timothy 4:11
312 . . . . Acts 15:1-21
313 . . . . Acts 15:40-16:15
314 . . . . Acts 16:16-40
315 . . . . Acts 17:1-15
316 . . . . Acts 17:16-34
317 . . . . Acts 18:1-17
318. . 1 Thessalonians 4:1-5:11
319 . . . . Acts 19:1-22

Day

320 .... 1 Corinthians 14
321 .... 1 Corinthians 13
322 .... 1 Corinthians 6
323 .... 1 Corinthians 5
324 . . 2 Corinthians 4:16-5:21
325 .... Acts 19:23-41
326 .... Acts 20:1-12
327 .... Acts 20:13-38
328......... Romans 3:9-31
329......... Romans 5:1-11
330............ Romans 12
331............. Romans 8
332............ Romans 14
333............ Galatians 5
334 .... Acts 21:1-14
335 .... Acts 21:17-36
336....... Acts 21:37-22:29
337 .... Acts 22:30-23:11
338 .... Acts 23:12-35
339 .... Acts 24
340 .... Acts 25:1-12
341....... Acts 25:23-26:32
342 .... Acts 27:1-12
343 .... Acts 27:13-44
344 .... Acts 28:1-10
345 .... Acts 28:11-31

Day

346....... Ephesians 2:1-10; 4:17-32
347 .... Colossians 3:1-4
348............. Philemon
349 ...... Philippians 2:1-18
350 ...... Hebrews 10:19-39

Day

351 .... Hebrews 11
352........... 1 Timothy 4
353....... 1 Timothy 6:3-19
354 .... Titus 2:11-3:8
355........... 2 Timothy 3
356....... 2 Timothy 4:6-22
357.......... James 1:19-27; 3:1-11; 4:11-12
358......... 1 Peter 2:13-3:9
359 .... 2 Peter 3
360 .... 1 John 3
361........... Revelation 3
362........... Revelation 4
363.......... Revelation 13
364...... Revelation 14:6-16
365.......... Revelation 20
366 .... Revelation 21:1-22:7

APPENDIX B

SPIRIT OF PROPHECY FIVE-YEAR READING PROGRAM

Messages to Young People (MYP) *Patriarchs and Prophets* (PP)

(Note: Read to end of last full paragraph on page listed, or to subheading.)

January

1. MYP 15-18
2. MYP 20-24
3. MYP 24-28
4. MYP 28-32
5. MYP 33-35
6. MYP 36-38
7. MYP 39-43
8. MYP 43-46
9. MYP 46-48
10. MYP 50-53
11. MYP 54-56
12. MYP 57-60
13. MYP 60-64
14. MYP 65-67
15. MYP 68-70
16. MYP 71-74
17. MYP 75-77
18. MYP 78-82
19. MYP 83-86
20. MYP 86-90
21. MYP 91-97
22. MYP 97-101
23. MYP 101-104
24. MYP 105-106
25. MYP 107-110
26. MYP 111-115
27. MYP 115-118
28. MYP 120-124
29. MYP 124-127
30. MYP 127-130
31. MYP 131-133

February

1. MYP 134-136
2. MYP 137-139
3. MYP 139-142
4. MYP 143-146
5. MYP 147-150
6. MYP 151-155
7. MYP 155-158
8. MYP 159-162
9. MYP 163-166
10. MYP 168-172
11. MYP 173-176
12. MYP 177-180
13. MYP 181-184
14. MYP 185-187
15. MYP 188-191
16. MYP 192-194
17. MYP 196-199
18. MYP 200-203
19. MYP 204-207
20. MYP 207-209
21. MYP 210-212
22. MYP 213-216
23. MYP 217-220
24. MYP 220-224
25. MYP 224-227
26. MYP 228-230
27. MYP 232-235
28. MYP 236-238

March

1. MYP 239-240
2. MYP 241-244
3. MYP 246-250
4. MYP 251-255
5. MYP 255-258
6. MYP 259-261
7. MYP 262-264
8. MYP 265-268
9. MYP 270-274
10. MYP 275-278
11. MYP 279-282
12. MYP 283-286
13. MYP 287-289
14. MYP 290-292
15. MYP 293-296
16. MYP 298-302
17. MYP 303-305
18. MYP 306-308
19. MYP 309-312
20. MYP 313-315
21. MYP 316-319
22. MYP 320-322
23. MYP 324-328

24. MYP 329-332
25. MYP 332-334
26. MYP 335-337
27. MYP 337-340
28. MYP 341-342
29. MYP 344-348
30. MYP 349-350
31. MYP 351-353

April

1. MYP 354-357
2. MYP 358-360
3. MYP 362-366
4. MYP 367-369
5. MYP 369-372
6. MYP 373-375
7. MYP 375-378
8. MYP 379-381
9. MYP 382-384
10. MYP 385-388
11. MYP 388-391
12. MYP 392-393
13. MYP 394-397
14. MYP 398-400
15. MYP 402-406
16. MYP 407-410
17. MYP 411-413
18. MYP 413-416
19. MYP 417-419
20. MYP 420-422
21. MYP 423-425
22. MYP 425-428
23. MYP 429-431
24. MYP 432-436
25. MYP 437-438
26. MYP 439-442
27. MYP 443-445
28. MYP 445-448
29. MYP 448-452
30. MYP 453-457

May

1. MYP 457-460
2. MYP 461-463
3. MYP 464-466
4. PP 33-35
5. PP 35-38
6. PP 38-40
7. PP 40-43
8. PP 44-46
9. PP 46-48
10. PP 48-51
11. PP 52-54
12. PP 54-57
13. PP 57-60
14. PP 60-62
15. PP 63-65
16. PP 65-67
17. PP 67-70
18. PP 71-73
19. PP 73-77
20. PP 78-79
21. PP 80-82
22. PP 82-84
23. PP 85-86
24. PP 86-89
25. PP 90-92
26. PP 92-97
27. PP 97-99
28. PP 99-101
29. PP 101-104
30. PP 105-107
31. PP 107-110

June

1. PP 111-113
2. PP 114-116
3. PP 117-119
4. PP 119-124
5. PP 125-126
6. PP 126-128
7. PP 129-131
8. PP 132-134
9. PP 134-136
10. PP 136-139
11. PP 139-142
12. PP 142-144
13. PP 145-147
14. PP 147-152
15. PP 153-155
16. PP 156-159
17. PP 159-162
18. PP 162-167
19. PP 167-170
20. PP 171-173
21. PP 173-176
22. PP 177-179
23. PP 180-182
24. PP 183-187
25. PP 187-190
26. PP 190-193
27. PP 193-196
28. PP 196-201
29. PP 201-203
30. PP 204-206

July

1. PP 206-209
2. PP 210-212
3. PP 213-217
4. PP 217-220
5. PP 220-223
6. PP 224-226
7. PP 226-228
8. PP 228-230
9. PP 230-232
10. PP 233-234
11. PP 234-237
12. PP 237-240
13. PP 241-243
14. PP 243-245
15. PP 245-247
16. PP 247-251

17. PP 251-253
18. PP 253-256
19. PP 257-258
20. PP 259-260
21. PP 260-264
22. PP 264-267
23. PP 267-269
24. PP 270-272
25. PP 273-277
26. PP 277-280
27. PP 281-283
28. PP 283-287
29. PP 287-290
30. PP 291-293
31. PP 293-296

August

1. PP 296-299
2. PP 299-302
3. PP 303-305
4. PP 305-307
5. PP 308-309
6. PP 309-311
7. PP 311-314
8. PP 315-317
9. PP 317-319
10. PP 320-324
11. PP 324-327
12. PP 327-330
13. PP 331-333
14. PP 333-336
15. PP 337-339
16. PP 339-342
17. PP 343-347
18. PP 347-350
19. PP 350-353
20. PP 353-356
21. PP 357-360
22. PP 360-362
23. PP 363-365
24. PP 365-368
25. PP 368-371
26. PP 371-373
27. PP 374-376
28. PP 376-379
29. PP 379-382
30. PP 382-386
31. PP 387-389

September

1. PP 389-392
2. PP 392-394
3. PP 395-397
4. PP 397-399
5. PP 399-402
6. PP 402-405
7. PP 406-408
8. PP 408-411
9. PP 412-414
10. PP 414-419
11. PP 420-423
12. PP 423-426
13. PP 426-429
14. PP 429-432
15. PP 433-435
16. PP 435-438
17. PP 439-441
18. PP 441-444
19. PP 447-449
20. PP 450-452
21. PP 453-455
22. PP 455-458
23. PP 458-461
24. PP 462-464
25. PP 464-468
26. PP 469-471
27. PP 471-476
28. PP 476-480
29. PP 481-483
30. PP 483-486

October

1. PP 487-491
2. PP 491-493
3. PP 493-495
4. PP 495-498
5. PP 499-503
6. PP 503-506
7. PP 506-509
8. PP 510-512
9. PP 512-514
10. PP 514-517
11. PP 517-520
12. PP 521-523
13. PP 523-526
14. PP 526-529
15. PP 530-532
16. PP 532-534
17. PP 534-536
18. PP 537-539
19. PP 539-542
20. PP 543-545
21. PP 545-547
22. PP 547-549
23. PP 549-554
24. PP 554-556
25. PP 556-559
26. PP 560-562
27. PP 563-565
28. PP 565-568
29. PP 569-571
30. PP 571-574
31. PP 575-577

November

1. PP 577-580
2. PP 581-583
3. PP 583-585
4. PP 585-588
5. PP 588-591
6. PP 592-594
7. PP 594-599

8. PP 599-602
9. PP 603-605
10. PP 605-607
11. PP 607-610
12. PP 610-612
13. PP 612-615
14. PP 616-618
15. PP 621-623
16. PP 624-626
17. PP 627-629
18. PP 629-631
19. PP 632-633
20. PP 633-636
21. PP 637-638
22. PP 641-642
23. PP 643-645
24. PP 645-647
25. PP 648-650
26. PP 650-652
27. PP 652-654
28. PP 654-656
29. PP 656-659
30. PP 660-662

DECEMBER

1. PP 662-665
2. PP 665-667
3. PP 667-671
4. PP 671-674
5. PP 675-679
6. PP 680-682
7. PP 683-685
8. PP 685-687
9. PP 687-690
10. PP 691-693
11. PP 693-696
12. PP 697-699
13. PP 699-702
14. PP 703-705
15. PP 705-708
16. PP 708-713
17. PP 713-716
18. PP 717-719
19. PP 719-721
20. PP 722-723
21. PP 723-726
22. PP 727-729
23. PP 729-731
24. PP 731-736
25. PP 736-739
26. PP 739-742
27. PP 742-745
28. PP 746-748
29. PP 748-750
30. PP 750-752
31. PP 752-755.

The Great Controversy (GC)
The Ministry of Healing (MH)

(Note: Read to end of last full paragraph on page listed, or to subheading.)

JANUARY

1. GC v-viii
2. GC ix-xii
3. GC 17-21
4. GC 21-27
5. GC 27-32
6. GC 32-38
7. GC 39-41
8. GC 41-44
9. GC 45-48
10. GC 49-51
11. GC 51-54
12. GC 54-57
13. GC 57-60
14. GC 61-63
15. GC 63-65
16. GC 65-68
17. GC 68-71
18. GC 71-73
19. GC 73-75
20. GC 75-78
21. GC 79-81
22. GC 82-83
23. GC 84-86
24. GC 86-89
25. GC 89-91
26. GC 91-93
27. GC 94-96
28. GC 97-100
29. GC 101-104
30. GC 104-107
31. GC 108-110

FEBRUARY

1. GC 110-113
2. GC 113-116
3. GC 116-119
4. GC 120-123
5. GC 123-126
6. GC 126-129
7. GC 129-133
8. GC 133-137
9. GC 137-140
10. GC 140-144
11. GC 145-147
12. GC 148-150
13. GC 150-153
14. GC 153-156
15. GC 156-159

16. GC 160-162
17. GC 162-165
18. GC 165-167
19. GC 167-170
20. GC 171-173
21. GC 174-176
22. GC 176-178
23. GC 178-181
24. GC 181-184
25. GC 185-189
26. GC 190-194
27. GC 195-198
28. GC 199-202

March

1. GC 203-207
2. GC 208-210
3. GC 211-214
4. GC 214-217
5. GC 217-221
6. GC 221-224
7. GC 224-228
8. GC 228-232
9. GC 232-236
10. GC 237-239
11. GC 239-242
12. GC 234-244
13. GC 245-247
14. GC 247-251
15. GC 251-254
16. GC 254-257
17. GC 257-260
18. GC 260-262
19. GC 262-264
20. GC 265-267
21. GC 267-270
22. GC 270-273
23. GC 273-276
24. GC 276-279
25. GC 279-282
26. GC 283-285
27. GC 285-288
28. GC 289-292
29. GC 292-295
30. GC 295-298
31. GC 299-301

April

1. GC 301-303
2. GC 303-305
3. GC 306-308
4. GC 308-311
5. GC 312-314
6. GC 315-316
7. GC 317-320
8. GC 320-324
9. GC 324-328
10. GC 328-332
11. GC 332-335
12. GC 335-339
13. GC 339-342
14. GC 343-345
15. GC 345-348
16. GC 348-351
17. GC 351-354
18. GC 355-358
19. GC 359-362
20. GC 363-366
21. GC 366-370
22. GC 370-374
23. GC 375-378
24. GC 378-381
25. GC 381-384
26. GC 384-387
27. GC 388-390
28. GC 391-393
29. GC 393-395
30. GC 395-397

May

1. GC 398-400
2. GC 400-402
3. GC 402-405
4. GC 405-408
5. GC 409-412
6. GC 412-415
7. GC 415-418
8. GC 418-422
9. GC 423-425
10. GC 425-428
11. GC 428-432
12. GC 433-435
13. GC 435-437
14. GC 437-439
15. GC 439-442
16. GC 442-445
17. GC 445-448
18. GC 448-450
19. GC 451-453
20. GC 453-457
21. GC 457-460
22. GC 461-463
23. GC 463-466
24. GC 466-468
25. GC 469-471
26. GC 472-475
27. GC 475-478
28. GC 479-481
29. GC 482-483
30. GC 483-486
31. GC 486-488

June

1. GC 488-491
2. GC 492-495
3. GC 495-497
4. GC 497-500
5. GC 500-502
6. GC 502-504
7. GC 505-507
8. GC 507-510
9. GC 511-513
10. GC 513-517

11. GC 518-520
12. GC 520-523
13. GC 523-525
14. GC 526-528
15. GC 528-530
16. GC 531-533
17. GC 533-536
18. GC 536-538
19. GC 539-541
20. GC 541-544
21. GC 544-547
22. GC 548-550
23. GC 551-553
24. GC 553-556
25. GC 556-559
26. GC 560-562
27. GC 563-565
28. GC 565-568
29. GC 568-571
30. GC 571-574

July

1. GC 574-578
2. GC 578-581
3. GC 582-584
4. GC 584-587
5. GC 587-589
6. GC 589-592
7. GC 593-595
8. GC 595-597
9. GC 597-600
10. GC 600-602
11. GC 603-606
12. GC 606-609
13. GC 609-612
14. GC 613-615
15. GC 615-618
16. GC 618-621
17. GC 622-625
18. GC 625-628
19. GC 628-631
20. GC 631-634
21. GC 635-637
22. GC 637-639
23. GC 639-642
24. GC 643-645
25. GC 645-647
26. GC 647-649
27. GC 649-652
28. GC 653-656
29. GC 657-661
30. GC 662-665
31. GC 665-668

August

1. GC 668-671
2. GC 671-674
3. GC 674-678
4. MH 17-21
5. MH 21-25
6. MH 25-28
7. MH 29-33
8. MH 34-39
9. MH 39-44
10. MH 45-50
11. MH 51-53
12. MH 54-56
13. MH 56-58
14. MH 59-62
15. MH 63-66
16. MH 67-70
17. MH 71-72
18. MH 73-79
19. MH 81-85
20. MH 86-90
21. MH 91-94
22. MH 95-99
23. MH 100-103
24. MH 104-108
25. MH 111-114
26. MH 114-117
27. MH 117-121
28. MH 121-124
29. MH 125-129
30. MH 129-133
31. MH 133-136

September

1. MH 139-143
2. MH 143-146
3. MH 146-148
4. MH 148-151
5. MH 151-154
6. MH 154-158
7. MH 158-160
8. MH 161-163
9. MH 163-166
10. MH 166-169
11. MH 171-173
12. MH 173-177
13. MH 177-179
14. MH 179-182
15. MH 183-185
16. MH 185-188
17. MH 188-192
18. MH 192-194
19. MH 194-196
20. MH 196-198
21. MH 198-200
22. MH 201-202
23. MH 203-205
24. MH 205-206
25. MH 206-208
26. MH 209-210
27. MH 211-213
28. MH 213-216
29. MH 219-221
30. MH 221-224

October

1. MH 225-228
2. MH 228-231
3. MH 231-233

4. MH 234-237
5. MH 237-240
6. MH 241-244
7. MH 244-247
8. MH 247-251
9. MH 251-256
10. MH 256-259
11. MH 261-264
12. MH 264-268
13. MH 271-274
14. MH 274-276
15. MH 277-280
16. MH 280-283
17. MH 283-286
18. MH 287-291
19. MH 291-294
20. MH 295-299
21. MH 299-301
22. MH 301-304
23. MH 305-307
24. MH 308-310
25. MH 311-314
26. MH 314-317
27. MH 318-320
28. MH 320-322
29. MH 323-324
30. MH 325-327
31. MH 327-330

NOVEMBER

1. MH 330-334
2. MH 334-335
3. MH 337-339
4. MH 340-342
5. MH 342-344
6. MH 344-346
7. MH 349-350
8. MH 351-352
9. MH 352-355
10. MH 356-359
11. MH 359-362
12. MH 363-365
13. MH 365-370
14. MH 371-373
15. MH 373-375
16. MH 375-378
17. MH 379-381
18. MH 381-383
19. MH 383-385
20. MH 385-387
21. MH 388-390
22. MH 390-392
23. MH 392-394
24. MH 395-398
25. MH 398-401
26. MH 401-404
27. MH 404-406
28. MH 409-412
29. MH 413-415
30. MH 416-418

DECEMBER

1. MH 418-421
2. MH 421-423
3. MH 423-426
4. MH 427-429
5. MH 429-432
6. MH 432-435
7. MH 435-438
8. MH 439-440
9. MH 441-443
10. MH 443-445
11. MH 445-448
12. MH 448-450
13. MH 451-454
14. MH 454-457
15. MH 458-461
16. MH 461-464
17. MH 464-466
18. MH 469-472
19. MH 472-475
20. MH 476-479
21. MH 479-482
22. MH 483-485
23. MH 485-487
24. MH 488-490
25. MH 491-493
26. MH 493-496
27. MH 497-500
28. MH 500-502
29. MH 503-506
30. MH 507-511
31. MH 512-516

The Desire of Ages (DA)
Early Writings (EW)

(Note: Read to end of last full paragraph on page listed, or to subheading.)

JANUARY

1. DA 19-21
2. DA 22-24
3. DA 24-26
4. DA 27-29
5. DA 29-32
6. DA 32-36
7. DA 37-44
8. DA 44-49

9. DA 50-55
10. DA 55-58
11. DA 59-62
12. DA 62-67
13. DA 68-71
14. DA 72-74
15. DA 75-77
16. DA 77-81
17. DA 81-83
18. DA 84-87
19. DA 87-89
20. DA 89-92
21. DA 97-99
22. DA 99-102
23. DA 102-105
24. DA 105-108
25. DA 109-111
26. DA 112-115
27. DA 115-118
28. DA 118-121
29. DA 122-123
30. DA 124-126
31. DA 126-131

February

1. DA 132-134
2. DA 134-137
3. DA 137-140
4. DA 140-143
5. DA 144-147
6. DA 147-150
7. DA 150-153
8. DA 154-156
9. DA 156-161
10. DA 161-164
11. DA 164-166
12. DA 167-171
13. DA 171-174
14. DA 174-177
15. DA 178-182
16. DA 183-187
17. DA 187-189
18. DA 190-192
19. DA 192-195
20. DA 196-198
21. DA 198-200
22. DA 201-203
23. DA 203-206
24. DA 207-209
25. DA 209-211
26. DA 211-213
27. DA 214-216
28. DA 216-219

March

1. DA 219-222
2. DA 222-225
3. DA 231-232
4. DA 232-235
5. DA 236-237
6. DA 237-240
7. DA 240-243
8. DA 244-245
9. DA 245-249
10. DA 249-251
11. DA 252-254
12. DA 254-256
13. DA 256-259
14. DA 259-261
15. DA 262-264
16. DA 264-266
17. DA 267-269
18. DA 269-271
19. DA 272-275
20. DA 275-278
21. DA 278-280
22. DA 281-283
23. DA 283-285
24. DA 285-287
25. DA 287-289
26. DA 290-292
27. DA 292-295
28. DA 295-297
29. DA 298-300
30. DA 300-305
31. DA 306-308

April

1. DA 309-311
2. DA 311-314
3. DA 315-317
4. DA 317-320
5. DA 321-323
6. DA 323-327
7. DA 328-329
8. DA 329-332
9. DA 333-335
10. DA 335-338
11. DA 338-341
12. DA 342-344
13. DA 344-348
14. DA 349-351
15. DA 351-354
16. DA 354-358
17. DA 359-361
18. DA 361-364
19. DA 365-368
20. DA 369-371
21. DA 372-376
22. DA 377-379
23. DA 380-382
24. DA 383-385
25. DA 385-388
26. DA 388-391
27. DA 391-394
28. DA 395-397
29. DA 397-400
30. DA 400-403

May

1. DA 404-406
2. DA 406-409
3. DA 410-412

4. DA 412-415
5. DA 415-418
6. DA 419-421
7. DA 421-425
8. DA 426-428
9. DA 428-431
10. DA 432-434
11. DA 434-436
12. DA 437-439
13. DA 439-442
14. DA 447-448
15. DA 448-451
16. DA 451-454
17. DA 455-457
18. DA 457-460
19. DA 460-463
20. DA 464-466
21. DA 466-469
22. DA 469-472
23. DA 472-475
24. DA 476-477
25. DA 478-479
26. DA 479-484
27. DA 485-486
28. DA 487-488
29. DA 488-493
30. DA 493-496
31. DA 497-500

June

1. DA 503-505
2. DA 506-507
3. DA 507-510
4. DA 511-515
5. DA 515-518
6. DA 518-523
7. DA 524-526
8. DA 526-529
9. DA 529-534
10. DA 535-538
11. DA 538-541
12. DA 547-548
13. DA 548-551
14. DA 552-556
15. DA 557-559
16. DA 560-564
17. DA 564-567
18. DA 567-570
19. DA 571-575
20. DA 575-579
21. DA 580-582
22. DA 582-584
23. DA 584-588
24. DA 589-592
25. DA 592-595
26. DA 595-598
27. DA 598-600
28. DA 601-603
29. DA 603-606
30. DA 606-609

July

1. DA 610-612
2. DA 612-615
3. DA 615-618
4. DA 618-620
5. DA 621-623
6. DA 624-626
7. DA 627-630
8. DA 630-633
9. DA 633-636
10. DA 637-639
11. DA 639-641
12. DA 642-644
13. DA 644-649
14. DA 650-651
15. DA 652-653
16. DA 653-655
17. DA 655-659
18. DA 660-661
19. DA 662-664
20. DA 664-668
21. DA 668-671
22. DA 671-673
23. DA 673-676
24. DA 676-678
25. DA 678-680
26. DA 685-686
27. DA 686-688
28. DA 688-690
29. DA 690-694
30. DA 694-697
31. DA 698-700

August

1. DA 700-705
2. DA 705-707
3. DA 707-709
4. DA 710-712
5. DA 712-715
6. DA 716-718
7. DA 719-720
8. DA 721-722
9. DA 723-725
10. DA 725-728
11. DA 729-731
12. DA 731-733
13. DA 733-735
14. DA 735-737
15. DA 738-740
16. DA 741-743
17. DA 743-746
18. DA 749-751
19. DA 751-755
20. DA 755-759
21. DA 759-762
22. DA 762-764
23. DA 769-771
24. DA 771-774
25. DA 774-777
26. DA 777-780
27. DA 781-786
28. DA 786-789

29. DA 789-794
30. DA 795-799
31. DA 799-801

September

1. DA 802-805
2. DA 805-808
3. DA 809-810
4. DA 810-812
5. DA 812-817
6. DA 818-820
7. DA 820-823
8. DA 823-825
9. DA 826-828
10. DA 829-830
11. DA 830-832
12. DA 832-835
13. EW 11-13
14. EW 13-16
15. EW 16-20
16. EW 20-22
17. EW 22-24
18. EW 32-33
19. EW 33-35
    (No.1) 85-86
20. EW 36-38
21. EW 39-41
22. EW 42-43
23. EW 43-45
24. EW 46-48
25. EW 48-50
26. EW 50-52
27. (No.6), 93-95
28. EW 52-54
29. EW 54-56,
    Note 5, 92-93
30. EW 56-58

October

1. EW 59-60
2. (No. 4), 86-89
3. EW 90-92
4. EW 61-64
5. EW 64-65
6. EW 65-67
7. EW 68-69
8. EW 69-71
9. EW 72-73
10. EW 74-76
11. EW 76-78
12. EW 78-81
13. EW 81-83
14. EW 96-98
15. EW 98-100
16. EW 100-102
17. EW 102-104
18. EW 104-107
19. EW 107-110
20. EW 111-114
21. EW 114-116
22. EW 116-118
23. EW 118-121
24. EW 121-122
25. EW 123-125
26. EW 125-127
27. EW 133-135
28. EW 135-137
29. EW 137-140
30. EW 140-143
31. EW 145-147

November

1. EW 147-149
2. EW 149-150
3. EW 150-153
4. EW 153-155
5. EW 155-158
6. EW 158-161
7. EW 162-164
8. EW 165-166
9. EW 167-168
10. EW 169-171
11. EW 171-173
12. EW 173-175
13. EW 176-178
14. EW 178-181
15. EW 181-184
16. EW 184-187
17. EW 187-190
18. EW 190-192
19. EW 192-194
20. EW 194-197
21. EW 197-199
22. EW 200-202
23. EW 202-205
24. EW 206-208
25. EW 208-211
26. EW 211-213
27. EW 213-215
28. EW 215-217
29. EW 218-219
30. EW 220-222

December

1. EW 222-224
2. EW 224-226
3. EW 226-228
4. EW 229-230
5. EW 230-232
6. EW 232-234
7. EW 235-237
8. EW 237-240
9. EW 240-242
10. EW 243-245
11. EW 245-247
12. EW 247-250
13. EW 250-252
14. EW 252-253
15. EW 254-256
16. EW 256-258
17. EW 258-261
18. EW 262-264
19. EW 264-266

20. EW 266-269
21. EW 269-271
22. EW 272-274
23. EW 274-276
24. EW 277-279
25. EW 279-282
26. EW 282-285
27. EW 285-287
28. EW 287-289
29. EW 289-291
30. EW 292-294
31. EW 294-295

Christ's Object Lessons (COL)
The Acts of the Apostles (AA)

(Note: Read to end of last full paragraph on page listed, or to subheading.)

January

1. COL 17-19
2. COL 19-21
3. COL 21-23
4. COL 24-26
5. COL 27-29
6. COL 29-31
7. COL 32-34
8. COL 35-37
9. COL 38-40
10. COL 41-43
11. COL 44-46
12. COL 47-49
13. COL 50-52
14. COL 53-55
15. COL 56-58
16. COL 59-61
17. COL 62-64
18. COL 65-67
19. COL 68-70
20. COL 71-73
21. COL 74-76
22. COL 77-79
23. COL 80-82
24. COL 83-85
25. COL 86-88
26. COL 89-91
27. COL 92-94
28. COL 95-97
29. COL 98-100
30. COL 101-103
31. COL 104-106

February

1. COL 107-109
2. COL 110-112
3. COL 113-115
4. COL 116-118
5. COL 119-121
6. COL 122-124
7. COL 125-127
8. COL 128-130
9. COL 131-133
10. COL 134-136
11. COL 137-139
12. COL 140-142
13. COL 143-145
14. COL 146-148
15. COL 149-151
16. COL 153-155
17. COL 156-158
18. COL 159-161
19. COL 162-164
20. COL 165-167
21. COL 168-170
22. COL 171-173
23. COL 174-176
24. COL 177-179
25. COL 180-182
26. COL 183-185
27. COL 186-188
28. COL 189-191

March

1. COL 192-194
2. COL 195-197
3. COL 198-200
4. COL 201-203
5. COL 204-206
6. COL 207-209
7. COL 210-212
8. COL 213-215
9. COL 216-218
10. COL 219-221
11. COL 222-224
12. COL 225-227
13. COL 228-230
14. COL 231-233
15. COL 234-236
16. COL 237-239
17. COL 240-242
18. COL 243-245
19. COL 246-248
20. COL 249-251
21. COL 252-254
22. COL 255-257
23. COL 258-260
24. COL 261-263
25. COL 264-266
26. COL 267-269
27. COL 270-272
28. COL 273-275
29. COL 276-278
30. COL 279-281

31. COL 282-284

April

1. COL 285-287
2. COL 288-290
3. COL 291-293
4. COL 294-296
5. COL 297-299
6. COL 300-302
7. COL 303-305
8. COL 306-308
9. COL 309-310
10. COL 311-313
11. COL 314-316
12. COL 317-319
13. COL 320-322
14. COL 323-325
15. COL 326-328
16. COL 329-331
17. COL 332-334
18. COL 335-337
19. COL 338-340
20. COL 341-343
21. COL 344-346
22. COL 347-349
23. COL 350-351
24. COL 352-354
25. COL 355-357
26. COL 358-360
27. COL 361-363
28. COL 364-366
29. COL 367-369
30. COL 370-372

May

1. COL 373-375
2. COL 376-378
3. COL 379-381
4. COL 382-385
5. COL 386-389
6. COL 390-393
7. COL 393-397
8. COL 397-400
9. COL 400-404
10. COL 405-408
11. COL 408-414
12. COL 414-417
13. COL 418-421
14. AA 9-11
15. AA 11-14
16. AA 14-16
17. AA 17-19
18. AA 19-21
19. AA 21-24
20. AA 25-27
21. AA 27-29
22. AA 29-31
23. AA 31-34
24. AA 35-37
25. AA 38-40
26. AA 41-43
27. AA 43-46
28. AA 47-50
29. AA 50-53
30. AA 53-56
31. AA 57-59

June

1. AA 59-61
2. AA 61-63
3. AA 63-66
4. AA 67-69
5. AA 70-72
6. AA 72-74
7. AA 74-76
8. AA 77-79
9. AA 79-82
10. AA 82-86
11. AA 87-89
12. AA 89-92
13. AA 92-94
14. AA 95-96
15. AA 97-98
16. AA 98-100
17. AA 100-102
18. AA 103-105
19. AA 105-108
20. AA 108-111
21. AA 112-114
22. AA 115-117
23. AA 117-120
24. AA 120-122
25. AA 123-125
26. AA 125-128
27. AA 128-130
28. AA 131-133
29. AA 133-136
30. AA 136-139

July

1. AA 139-142
2. AA 143-145
3. AA 145-148
4. AA 149-151
5. AA 151-154
6. AA 155-157
7. AA 158-160
8. AA 160-162
9. AA 162-165
10. AA 166-168
11. AA 169-171
12. AA 171-173
13. AA 173-176
14. AA 177-179
15. AA 179-182
16. AA 182-184
17. AA 184-187
18. AA 188-190
19. AA 190-193
20. AA 193-195
21. AA 195-197
22. AA 197-200
23. AA 201-203

24. AA 203-205
25. AA 205-207
26. AA 207-210
27. AA 211-213
28. AA 213-216
29. AA 217-220
30. AA 221-222
31. AA 223-224

August

1. AA 224-226
2. AA 226-228
3. AA 228-230
4. AA 231-233
5. AA 233-235
6. AA 235-237
7. AA 237-239
8. AA 239-242
9. AA 243-245
10. AA 245-247
11. AA 247-249
12. AA 250-251
13. AA 251-254
14. AA 255-257
15. AA 257-259
16. AA 259-261
17. AA 261-263
18. AA 263-265
19. AA 265-268
20. AA 269-271
21. AA 271-274
22. AA 274-277
23. AA 277-280
24. AA 281-283
25. AA 283-285
26. AA 285-288
27. AA 288-290
28. AA 291-293
29. AA 294-297
30. AA 298-300
31. AA 300-303

September

1. AA 303-305
2. AA 305-308
3. AA 309-311
4. AA 311-314
5. AA 314-317
6. AA 317-319
7. AA 319-322
8. AA 323-325
9. AA 325-327
10. AA 327-329
11. AA 330-332
12. AA 332-334
13. AA 335-337
14. AA 337-340
15. AA 340-343
16. AA 343-345
17. AA 346-348
18. AA 348-350
19. AA 350-352
20. AA 352-355
21. AA 355-358
22. AA 359-361
23. AA 361-363
24. AA 363-365
25. AA 365-368
26. AA 368-371
27. AA 372-374
28. AA 375-377
29. AA 377-379
30. AA 379-382

October

1. AA 383-384
2. AA 384-386
3. AA 386-388
4. AA 389-391
5. AA 391-393
6. AA 393-395
7. AA 395-398
8. AA 399-401
9. AA 402-404
10. AA 404-406
11. AA 406-408
12. AA 408-410
13. AA 410-412
14. AA 412-415
15. AA 415-418
16. AA 419-421
17. AA 421-423
18. AA 423-425
19. AA 425-427
20. AA 428-430
21. AA 430-432
22. AA 433-434
23. AA 434-436
24. AA 436-438
25. AA 439-440
26. AA 440-442
27. AA 443-444
28. AA 444-446
29. AA 447-448
30. AA 448-450
31. AA 450-452

November

1. AA 452-454
2. AA 454-456
3. AA 457-458
4. AA 458-460
5. AA 461-463
6. AA 463-465
7. AA 465-468
8. AA 469-470
9. AA 470-472
10. AA 473-474
11. AA 474-476
12. AA 476-478
13. AA 479-480
14. AA 480-482
15. AA 482-484
16. AA 485-486

17. AA 486-488
18. AA 489-491
19. AA 492-493
20. AA 493-495
21. AA 495-497
22. AA 498-500
23. AA 500-503
24. AA 503-505
25. AA 505-508
26. AA 509-511
27. AA 511-513
28. AA 514-516
29. AA 516-519
30. AA 519-522

December

1. AA 515-525
2. AA 525-528
3. AA 529-531
4. AA 532-533
5. AA 534-536
6. AA 536-538
7. AA 539-541
8. AA 541-543
9. AA 543-545
10. AA 546-548
11. AA 548-551
12. AA 551-553
13. AA 554-556
14. AA 557-559
15. AA 560-562
16. AA 562-564
17. AA 565-567
18. AA 568-570
19. AA 570-572
20. AA 572-574
21. AA 574-577
22. AA 578-580
23. AA 580-583
24. AA 583-585
25. AA 586-587
26. AA 588-590
27. AA 590-592
28. AA 593-595
29. AA 595-597
30. AA 597-600
31. AA 601-602

Christian Service (CS)
Prophets and Kings (PK)

(Note: Read to end of last full paragraph on page listed, or to subheading.)

January

1. CS 7-9
2. CS 10-12
3. CS 13-15
4. CS 16-18
5. CS 19-21
6. CS 22-24
7. CS 25-27
8. CS 28-30
9. CS 31-33
10. CS 34-36
11. CS 37-39
12. CS 40-42
13. CS 43-45
14. CS 46-48
15. CS 49-51
16. CS 52-54
17. CS 55-57
18. CS 58-60
19. CS 61-63
20. CS 64-66
21. CS 67-69
22. CS 70-72
23. CS 73-75
24. CS 76-78
25. CS 79-81
26. CS 82-84
27. CS 85-87
28. CS 88-90
29. CS 91-93
30. CS 92-94
31. CS 95-97

February

1. CS 98-100
2. CS 101-103
3. CS 104-106
4. CS 107-109
5. CS 110-112
6. CS 113-115
7. CS 116-118
8. CS 119-121
9. CS 122-124
10. CS 125-126
11. CS 127-128
12. CS 129-131
13. CS 132-134
14. CS 135-137
15. CS 138-140
16. CS 141-143
17. CS 144-146
18. CS 147-149
19. CS 150-152
20. CS 153-154

21. CS 155-157
22. CS 158-160
23. CS 161-163
24. CS 164-166
25. CS 167-169
26. CS 170-172
27. CS 173-175
28. CS 176-177

March

1. CS 178-180
2. CS 181-183
3. CS 184-186
4. CS 187-189
5. CS 190-192
6. CS 193-195
7. CS 196-198
8. CS 199-201
9. CS 202-204
10. CS 205-207
11. CS 208-210
12. CS 212-214
13. CS 215-217
14. CS 218-220
15. CS 221-223
16. CS 224-226
17. CS 227-229
18. CS 230-232
19. CS 233-235
20. CS 236-238
21. CS 239-241
22. CS 242-244
23. CS 246-248
24. CS 249-251
25. CS 253-255
26. CS 257-259
27. CS 260-262
28. CS 263-265
29. CS 266-268
30. CS 270-272
31. CS 273-275

April

1. PK 15-16
2. PK 17-18
3. PK 19-20
4. PK 21-22
5. PK 23-24
6. PK 25-26
7. PK 27-28
8. PK 29-30
9. PK 31-32
10. PK 33-34
11. PK 35-36
12. PK 37-38
13. PK 39-40
14. PK 41-42
15. PK 43-44
16. PK 45-46
17. PK 47-48
18. PK 49-50
19. PK 51-52
20. PK 53-54
21. PK 55-56
22. PK 57-58
23. PK 59-60
24. PK 61-62
25. PK 63-64
26. PK 65-66
27. PK 67-68
28. PK 69-70
29. PK 71-72
30. PK 73-74

May

1. PK 75-76
2. PK 77-78
3. PK 79-80
4. PK 81-82
5. PK 83-84
6. PK 85-86
7. PK 87-88
8. PK 89-90
9. PK 91-92
10. PK 93-94
11. PK 95-96
12. PK 97-98
13. PK 99-100
14. PK 101-102
15. PK 103-104
16. PK 105-106
17. PK 107-108
18. PK 109-110
19. PK 111-112
20. PK 113-114
21. PK 115-116
22. PK 117-118
23. PK 119-120
24. PK 121-122
25. PK 123-124
26. PK 125-126
27. PK 127-128
28. PK 129-130
29. PK 131-132
30. PK 133-134
31. PK 135-136

June

1. PK 137-138
2. PK 139-140
3. PK 141-142
4. PK 143-144
5. PK 145-146
6. PK 147-148
7. PK 149-150
8. PK 151-152
9. PK 153-154
10. PK 155-156
11. PK 157-158
12. PK 159-160
13. PK 161-162
14. PK 163-164
15. PK 165-166
16. PK 167-168

17. PK 169-170
18. PK 171-172
19. PK 173-174
20. PK 175-176
21. PK 177-178
22. PK 179-180
23. PK 181-182
24. PK 183-184
25. PK 185-186
26. PK 187-188
27. PK 189-190
28. PK 191-192
29. PK 193-194
30. PK 195-196

JULY

1. PK 197-198
2. PK 199-200
3. PK 201-202
4. PK 203-204
5. PK 205-206
6. PK 207-208
7. PK 209-210
8. PK 211-212
9. PK 213-214
10. PK 215-216
11. PK 217-218
12. PK 219-220
13. PK 221-222
14. PK 223-224
15. PK 225-226
16. PK 227-228
17. PK 229-230
18. PK 231-233
19. PK 234-236
20. PK 237-239
21. PK 240-242
22. PK 243-245
23. PK 246-248
24. PK 249-251
25. PK 252-254
26. PK 255-257
27. PK 258-260
28. PK 261-263
29. PK 264-266
30. PK 267-269
31. PK 270-272

AUGUST

1. PK 273-275
2. PK 276-278
3. PK 279-281
4. PK 282-284
5. PK 285-287
6. PK 288-300
7. PK 301-303
8. PK 304-306
9. PK 307-309
10. PK 310-312
11. PK 313-315
12. PK 316-318
13. PK 319-321
14. PK 322-324
15. PK 325-327
16. PK 328-330
17. PK 331-333
18. PK 334-336
19. PK 337-339
20. PK 340-342
21. PK 343-345
22. PK 346-348
23. PK 349-351
24. PK 352-354
25. PK 355-357
26. PK 358-360
27. PK 361-363
28. PK 364-366
29. PK 367-369
30. PK 370-372
31. PK 374-376

SEPTEMBER

1. PK 377-379
2. PK 380-382
3. PK 384-386
4. PK 387-389
5. PK 390-391
6. PK 392-394
7. PK 395-396
8. PK 397-398
9. PK 399-401
10. PK 402-404
11. PK 405-407
12. PK 408-410
13. PK 411-413
14. PK 414-416
15. PK 417-419
16. PK 420-422
17. PK 423-425
18. PK 426-428
19. PK 429-431
20. PK 432-434
21. PK 435-437
22. PK 438-439
23. PK 441-443
24. PK 444-446
25. PK 447-449
26. PK 450-452
27. PK 453-455
28. PK 456-458
29. PK 459-461
30. PK 462-464

OCTOBER

1. PK 465-467
2. PK 468-470
3. PK 471-473
4. PK 474-476
5. PK 477-479
6. PK 480-481
7. PK 482-484
8. PK 485-487
9. PK 488-490

10. PK 491-493
11. PK 494-496
12. PK 497-499
13. PK 500-502
14. PK 503-505
15. PK 506-508
16. PK 509-511
17. PK 512-514
18. PK 515-517
19. PK 518-520
20. PK 521-523
21. PK 524-526
22. PK 527-529
23. PK 530-531
24. PK 532-535
25. PK 536-538
26. PK 539-541
27. PK 542-544
28. PK 545-547
29. PK 548-550
30. PK 551-553
31. PK 554-556

NOVEMBER

1. PK 557-559
2. PK 560-562
3. PK 563-565
4. PK 566-568
5. PK 569-571
6. PK 572-574
7. PK 575-577
8. PK 578-580
9. PK 581-583
10. PK 584-586
11. PK 587-589
12. PK 590-592
13. PK 593-595
14. PK 596-598
15. PK 599-601
16. PK 602-604
17. PK 605-607
18. PK 608-610
19. PK 611-613
20. PK 614-616
21. PK 617-619
22. PK 620-622
23. PK 623-625
24. PK 626-628
25. PK 629-631
26. PK 632-634
27. PK 635-637
28. PK 638-640
29. PK 641-643
30. PK 644-646

DECEMBER

1. PK 647-649
2. PK 650-652
3. PK 653-655
4. PK 656-658
5. PK 659-661
6. PK 662-664
7. PK 665-667
8. PK 668-670
9. PK 672-674
10. PK 675-677
11. PK 678-680
12. PK 682-684
13. PK 685-687
14. PK 688-690
15. PK 691-693
16. PK 694-696
17. PK 698-700
18. PK 701-703
19. PK 704-706
20. PK 707-709
21. PK 710-711
22. PK 712-713
23. PK 714-715
24. PK 716-717
25. PK 718-719
26. PK 720-721
27. PK 722-723
28. PK 724-725
29. PK 726-727
30. PK 728-729
31. PK 730-733

APPENDIX C

Spiritual Emphasis Study Plan for Churches and Pastors

PASTORS

Pastors can motivate church members to read the Bible and Spirit of Prophecy by setting an example for them to follow. It is therefore

Recommended:

- That pastors be encouraged to spend more time each day reading Scripture and the Spirit of Prophecy to feed their own souls.
- That pastors be encouraged to listen to the reading of the Bible and the Spirit of Prophecy on tapes as they travel between appointments.
- That pastors be encouraged to listen to good expository sermons on tapes as they travel between appointments, e.g., a tape of the month club.
- That pastors experiment with opening up passages of Scripture for their congregations by doing more expository preaching.
- That pastors be encouraged to attend continuing education seminars on preaching.
- Pastors should be encouraged to reread *Testimonies to Ministers, Pastoral Ministry,* and *Evangelism* periodically.

LOCAL CONGREGATIONS

Pastors should encourage their congregations in the use of the Bible and the Spirit of Prophecy during the worship service. It is therefore

Recommended:

- That families be encouraged to bring their Bibles to church once again and follow Bible passages as they are read from the pulpit.
- That pew Bibles be provided where congregations so desire, thus encouraging everyone in the congregation to use the

Bible during the worship service.

- That pastors train local elders to read Scripture meaningfully during worship services.
- That pastors train their congregations in various methods of responsive reading from Scripture.
- That a Spirit of Prophecy quotation that relates to the sermon topic be printed in the church bulletin. The quotation could be read publicly sometime during the worship service.
- That references to additional Spirit of Prophecy statements that pertain to the sermon be printed in the church bulletin.
- That time be given to members for testimonies regarding biblical verses or Spirit of Prophecy passages that have brought them a blessing during the previous week.
- That reading groups that read chapters or entire small books from the Bible, with little or no commentary, be started. When a passage or book is finished, members of the group may then share their insights and impressions.
- That consideration be given to inductive reading of the Bible.

LOCAL CONFERENCES

Local conferences should facilitate a return to the study of the Bible and the Spirit of Prophecy.

Recommended:

- That conferences be encouraged to challenge pastors to do more expository preaching.
- That recordings of exceptionally good expository sermons given by local pastors be duplicated and circulated.
- That pastors' meetings occasionally be devoted to Bible-based expository preaching.
- That conferences be encouraged to choose one Ellen G. White (EGW) book a year and send discount coupons to members for the purchase of that book at the conference Adventist Book Center (ABC).
- That conferences be encouraged to give each newly baptized member a discount coupon for the purchase of an EGW book of their choice at the conference ABC. The coupon could be enclosed in the letter sent by the conference president to all new members at the time they are welcomed into the conference family.

- That conferences be encouraged to include demonstrations showing the power of properly reading Scripture publicly at pastors' meetings and teachers' conventions.
- That better communication be established with church members about discount promotions on Spirit of Prophecy books (such as the October "Spirit of Prophecy Month" annual discount program). New members especially need to be informed about special discount promotions.
- That discounts on Spirit of Prophecy books be linked directly to study programs. Having a printed study guide booklet to accompany promoted Spirit of Prophecy books may actually help some people read the books they have purchased.

SABBATH SCHOOL LESSON QUARTERLY

Because the study of the weekly Sabbath school lesson is the only serious Bible study that many of our people do throughout the week, and because only a thorough knowledge of Scripture and of the counsel found in the Spirit of Prophecy will enable people to stand firm for truth in the face of the most cunning deceptions at the close of the great controversy, it is

Recommended:

- That all church members be encouraged to participate in daily lesson study.
- That one additional page of pertinent EGW quotes be added at the end of each lesson. These quotes can be identified with the daily study to which they relate. This page is not to replace the use of EGW quotes within the text of the weekly lesson, nor the suggested reading from the Spirit of Prophecy at the beginning of Friday's lesson. While the statement "Adult Sabbath School Bible Study Guide" has been added to the cover of the adult quarterly, the use of Spirit of Prophecy quotes are considered as tools to be used within this guide.
- That consideration be given to using an expository format for the study of the Bible at least two out of the four quarters each year. As a rule the format for each weekly study is topical, and this may be necessary for the study of some subjects. With an expository format, Sabbath school members would benefit from in-depth study of biblical passages.

SABBATH SCHOOL CLASSES

As far as the adult Sabbath school program is concerned, we are counseled that it should become the main thrust for soul winning. In hopes of helping to foster deeper study and application of the principles found in the Bible and the Spirit of Prophecy, the following is

Recommended:

- That the North American Division (NAD) support the Sabbath school action format for conducting the adult Sabbath school program. This small group format would not only encourage greater participation by class members in discussing the Bible as covered in that week's lesson, but also mobilize each adult class for the nurturing of its members, reclamation of missing members, and soul winning.
- That several specific union conferences be invited to pilot this project and develop a promotional strategy to bring this plan to the attention of all NAD churches.

APPENDIX D

Spiritual Emphasis Study Plan for Elementary, Secondary, and Higher Education

In an effort to challenge our educators to a deeper, prayerful study of the Bible and the Spirit of Prophecy, it is

Recommended:

- That educators be encouraged to spend more time each day reading the Scriptures and the Spirit of Prophecy to feed their own souls.
- That educators be encouraged to reread *Education, Fundamentals of Christian Education,* and *Counsels to Parents, Teachers, and Students* periodically.
- That educators be encouraged to listen to audio recordings

of the Bible and the Spirit of Prophecy in their car or home.

- That a special Spirit of Prophecy discount incentive program for educators be implemented. It could be jointly underwritten by the union conference, local ABC, and the publishing houses.
- That faculty members be encouraged to team up with other faculty members to pray for students and themselves.
- That all teachers be encouraged to pray with their students, as well as open each class with prayer.
- That all schools be encouraged to have faculty worship each morning, which should include reading and discussing of the Scriptures and the Spirit of Prophecy.

ELEMENTARY AND SECONDARY SCHOOL CLASSROOMS

In the hope of encouraging teachers to motivate their students to read the Bible and the Spirit of Prophecy, it is

Recommended:

- That teachers be encouraged to train students on how to read Scripture meaningfully in public.
- That teachers train stúdents in various methods of responsive reading from Scripture.
- That the Bible and Spirit of Prophecy be used more in the formal curriculum so that teachers will utilize these vital resources in their classrooms.
- That more Spirit of Prophecy and books about Ellen White be used as assigned reading for students.
- That appropriate Bible- and Spirit of Prophecy-related interactive CDs and videos be used in classroom presentations.
- That Spirit of Prophecy books be paraphrased for children and youth to understand them, such as was done in composing *Steps to Jesus* (an adaptation of *Steps to Christ*). Suggested books to begin with would include *The Desire of Ages, The Great Controversy, Thoughts From the Mount of Blessing,* and *Christ's Object Lessons.* Consideration should be given to dividing *The Desire of Ages* and *The Great Controversy* into three or four volumes each to make them more reader-friendly.
- That youth study guides for the above adapted Spirit of Prophecy books, for teachers to use, be prepared.

- That a study guide to accompany the *Keepers of the Flame* video series be prepared.
- That parents be encouraged to give Spirit of Prophecy books to their children at each birthday and Christmas along with their other gifts. Young people will read them more if they have their own personal books, and if parents continue giving, they will soon have a complete library of their own.
- That historical Adventist sites be included on school-sponsored field trips.

COLLEGE AND UNIVERSITY CLASSROOMS

In the hope of encouraging professors to motivate their students to read the Bible and the Spirit of Prophecy, it is

Recommended:

- That age-appropriate editions (i.e., vocabulary and illustrations) of the most widely circulated Spirit of Prophecy books be prepared for use by college and university students.
- That reference to Bible texts or Spirit of Prophecy quotations appropriate to the topic under discussion be included in class lectures.
- That when appropriate to the topic, assignments from Spirit of Prophecy books be included on collateral reading lists.
- That helpful explanatory background information regarding the Bible and Spirit of Prophecy be included in class discussions.
- That appropriate Bible- and Spirit of Prophecy-related interactive CDs and videos be utilized in classroom presentations.
- That historical Adventist sites be included on school-sponsored academic study trips.

APPENDIX E

Spiritual Emphasis Study Plan for Individuals and Families

The need for daily individual and family spiritual nourishment should once again be emphasized. In an effort to encourage our members in the prayerful study of the Bible and the Spirit of Prophecy, it is

Recommended:

- That the highest priority be given to urging once again that every Adventist family have daily family worship, with the importance and value of morning and evening family worship being stressed.
- That families be encouraged to set specific times for morning and evening family worship, recognizing that this may necessitate some changes in the schedules of individual family members in order to meet this crucial spiritual priority.
- That materials presenting an Adventist perspective on how to conduct family worship be utilized.
- That during family worship families be encouraged to pray not only for their own individual and family needs, but also for the needs of their own local congregation as well as for the extended work of the Adventist Church worldwide.
- That families be encouraged to study the Sabbath school lesson daily, including the appropriate materials that have been prepared specifically for children and youth. This may be done as part of the morning or evening family worship, or at some other time during the day.
- That all members be encouraged to spend quality personal time each day studying the Bible and the Spirit of Prophecy, in addition to daily family worship. It is recognized that the amount of time available for this personal study will vary depending upon each individual's daily schedule.
- That members be encouraged to make use of the various devotional books prepared each year by the church. Every fall these books are made available to churches at discounted prices. This fact could be mentioned by pastors when stressing the importance of family and individual devotions in their churches.